Habits For Success and Significance

7 Secrets To Accomplish Whatever You Want in Business, Time-Management, Mindset, Social Skills, and Entrepreneurship Strategies Included.

By Randy Wagner

ISBN (eBook): 978-1-955553-07-0
ISBN (Paperback): 978-1-955553-06-3
ISBN (Hardback): 978-1-955553-08-7
 Library of Congress Cataloging: 2021919070
Cover Design by Divine Grace Reyman
Printed in the United States of America
Visit the author's website at: **www.randybwagner.com**

Legal Notice:

Disclaimer Notice:

Table Of Contents

Contents

INTRODUCTION

"Depending on what they are, our habits will either make us or break us. We become what we repeatedly do." - Sean Covey.

Whenever we wake in the morning, irrespective of the level of success we've previously attained, we always think either briefly or elaborately about achieving success in a particular aspect (s) of our lives — be it financially, in our personal life, career, spiritually, etc. Whatever it is, success is something we all crave. We all want to be seen as successful. Why not? Of course, success makes us happy. No one wants to be identified with a failure. Success makes us feel good. It motivates us. People like to associate with us. It skyrockets our motivation to achieve more successes and improves our physical and mental state.

You will probably be able to write an endless list of successful people if asked to. But the question is: *"will you include your name as someone successful?"* The task here can make you ask yourself, if the people I write are successful, am I also successful? Is there something they know I am unaware of? Is there a way of life they live I haven't noticed yet? Is there a way they approach life that I don't? Lots and lots of such questions might come to your mind if given that task.

However, it is essential to note that "success" means different things to different people. What you count as success may not be for me. For instance, I may see success as giving relief materials to the war-affected populace in Syria, which I believe will make them feel not forgotten, while you can see success as having at least 40 million dollars in your account before clocking 40. It varies. My point is: there is no static definition of success, and there is no one type of successful person.

By my standard, I consider myself a success after achieving my financial freedom goals and becoming a writer and an entrepreneur. JK Rowling will probably define success to you based on her experience living in penury, being a single mother, who was on government aid, then writing Harry Potter, and becoming the best-selling living author in Britain. In the same vein, Col. Sanders, who has held several jobs in his early life, could consider his success as franchising KFC as a retiree at 62. Introduction Also, Jay Z, among the highest-grossing hip-hop artists, could tell you that his success is defined as acquiring wealth legally and stopping the sale of crack and cocaine. So, what am I driving at? Many people with different backgrounds and experiences will indeed define success to you differently.

You must, however, note that as much as there are different definitions of success, these definitions have a meeting point. You will find qualities in successful people that you won't find in someone who is doing not too well. There is no one way to succeed, but certain qualities are required to increase your chances of success.

Are there some lessons you can learn from successful people to guide and increase your chances of success? Do you want to know how you can effectively deal with failure? Do you want to overcome feeling envious of a family member or friend who seems to have figured everything out? Or do you feel left behind by others who are more successful than you? Are you ready to permanently silence the fear of wasting your life and not living up to your full potential? Are you worried that there are things that could hold you back from your goals? Are there hints to note that can make you know what you would like to become in the future? Or do you even know what you would like to develop but don't know how to achieve it? Put your mind at rest; these questions—including many others — will be discussed in this book.

You are not alone in the dark world of "unsuccessful trials." Many people all over the world are in the same situation as you. In fact, the larger population of the world is in this situation, which explains why many people will do anything to become successful. Here is the good news: you can achieve success in whatever area you wish. Wherever you walk in, you can command respect and attention. You can live the type of life you have always desired. Whatever you do, you can be the best. You can live your life to the fullest and do lots more. My testimony is a living testimony. I will share my story with you.

I was born in New York City to a family of 5. I am the first child with two other siblings (Sarah and Shawn). My father worked in a plastics factory full time, while my mum, suffering from acute back pain, worked as a babysitter. The nominal wages my parent got from their work was what they used to pay our monthly rent and my mum's medical bill. We don't need anyone to tell us (myself and my siblings) that they can't afford to send us to college or give us the life we desire. To sum it up, we were living in lack. Those were the trying periods of my life. To add to the family income, I had to pick up a shift job at a restaurant down our street. My sibling, too, followed suit. That wasn't the life we wanted. I constantly felt depressed, dejected, and suffered from low self-esteem. But will those feelings solve our problems? No! Then I rewrote the story of my family.

I was determined to live a life of financial freedom. My family is what I want to cater to. I want to go to college, and I want my siblings too to go. I want my family to live a life of abundance.

Those were the goals I wrote on the paper for myself. Having made those goals, now, how do I go about achieving them? I started by reading and learning about financial freedom. I visited libraries, reading everything on financial independence and other success books I could lay my hands on. Thereon, I started gaining insight into financial freedom; I gained marketable skills and started practicing some tips mentioned by the authors of the books I have read, then I started noticing changes in my quality of life.

I also followed some financial principles. I started sticking to my budgets. Through my savings, I created another source of income by supplying coffees to private and public organizations, and rigorously controlled my spending. Although it wasn't easy, I persevered and was determined throughout the challenges.

The selling of coffee boosted my financial position immeasurably. I must mention that passive income is a great way to increase your wealth, but it is not free money. You'll need to work for it and plan. The methods I've applied, which would later be discussed in this book, are excellent ways of building passive income, but all of them may vary in terms of the activity required upfront and passivity you can expect.

As days went by, I started feeling hopeful about life, my confidence level started growing, and I could pay my bills and cater for my parents and sibling. Now, we are all done with college. My siblings consult for organizations, and I can fulfill my ambition of becoming a financial investor, entrepreneur, and professional writer. I have taken on other challenges and am on the path to achieving them.

You can also experience similar testimony.

Who is this book for?

This book is for you if you want to reach your full potential. You will need this book if your image and prestige matter to you. It is a must-have for you if you are an aspiring entrepreneur or an entrepreneur—especially if you are between 20 to 40. If you also believe that you have to work for everything and that nothing can be handed to you, this book is a must-have for you. This book can serve as a guide if you want to rank fast in your organization. If people's success easily inspired you, you need to copy this book. All these and more are some reasons you need to have this book on your shelf.

From chapter one, I will take you through how habit defines your life. This chapter will explore why habits matter and are essential in achieving your goals. This chapter will also focus on how habit is the foundation of success, the definition of success, and how habit has made some people very successful, including how habits are developed, and tips for creating and sticking to good habits.

In chapter two, we will look at the unproductive and counterproductive habits and the ones that keep you from achieving success. This chapter will also center on breaking bad habits, procrastinating, overcoming self-defeating beliefs, staying in your comfort zone, and how mindfulness will help you break bad habits.

Chapter 3 explores the inner traits that most successful people have in common. Even though successful people come from different races and environments, you will find some unique characteristics that you must emulate. This is the target of this page.

The goal of chapter 4 will be about the importance of how you think and how that manifest into your life, how your mindset determines if you are going to be successful or not, the difference between fixed and growth mindset, and tips for upgrading or improving your mindset.

Chapter 5 will discuss how to set goals for yourself and know what you're working towards. You will be exposed to the importance of dreams in this chapter. You will also be introduced to examples of successful people who used goals to achieve success, set goals, and the habits to practice achieving your goals.

Chapter 6 will discuss why a consistent quality in your output is essential to success, why consistency is difficult, what character involves, what to keep in mind about consistency, and habits to practice and build consistency.

The importance of always looking for a solution and not giving up, no matter how large a problem or obstacle may seem, is being examined in chapter 7. The chapter further looks at how a solution-based approach is critical to achieving success. It also offers ways to be creative, strategies for solving problems strategically, and tips to help you nurture solution-based thinking.

The focus of Chapter 8 is to discuss the importance of social skills and how to deal with people from different walks of life. You are made to understand that you need others to succeed in any of your endeavors. The importance of social skills is also noted in this chapter, including ways you can improve your social skills. It further counsels on how social skills can help you build essential relationships that will help your success, and last, on the habits you need to inculcate to practice your social skills.

Chapter 9 reveals the importance of managing your time well and protecting it from being used up by others, how time management is an essential factor for success, applying the Pareto principle, how to say no, how to eliminate distraction, time boxing, and habits to practice ensuring that you can manage your time effectively.

The last chapter, which is chapter 10, uncovers the importance of giving back and helping others and knowing it's not just all about you. This is chapter discusses how giving back can contribute to your success, tips to help you give back, plus the habits to practice to that effect.

Last, my extensive research and experience about the subject have positioned me to offer strategies, approaches, and ways to develop the habits to make you successful. When you are done reading this book, one thing is sure: you will notice a considerable difference in your habits and be more conscious. I will advise that you take the techniques, tips, practical guides, and steps offered in this book seriously, as just reading without action may not bring any change. *"Action is the foundational element of success."* as Pablo Picasso once said.

Chapter1: Your Habits Define Your Life

"Sow an act, and you reap a habit. Sow a habit, and you reap a character. Sow a character, and you reap a destiny."–Charles Reade.

Have you tried reducing your weight, but proved impossible? Or perhaps you've attempted to reading everything you could lay your hands on about reducing weight, but all proved futile? Does this sound like part of your ordeal? Have you ever asked yourself why things didn't turn out the way you wanted? I will tell you why. You can eat healthily and run a marathon for a day, but you won't be able to reach your goal unless you stay consistent with a healthy habit. This is where the importance of habit comes in. You may not achieve your goals if you haven't inculcated the practices that will enable you to achieve them. All the successful people you know all have habits that facilitate their success. So why won't you want to learn about these habits? But first, let's understand the importance of habits:

Habits Are More Important Than You Realize

Can you imagine how stinking you would smell if you didn't regularly shower or brush your teeth? Thanks to the fact that you have cultivated the habit of constantly waking up daily to brush and bath, you exposed the world to air pollution. This is how vital habit is, but you never realize it. If you are wallowing in mediocrity, it means you have an accumulated behavioral debt that you need to work on.

By nature, we are all creatures of habits. According to a statistic, 45% of daily activities are habitual and automatic with little thought. We are inherently incapable of knowing how prevalent and influential they are because habits occur outside the spectrum of opinion. As soon as something becomes a habit, it doesn't require much thought and becomes automatic.

When I cut my spending, to have some money to fall back on, in my time of need, I said to myself that the questions that will decide if I need to spend on something will be: *"How much is this item?" "How important is the item in enabling achieve financial freedom?" "What is the value of this item in the short, medium, and long time?" Is there a substitute for this item that won't cost me that much, or no money at all?*. As I asked myself these questions and ingrained them in me as a habit, it made me develop the habit of asking critical questions whenever I am about to decide. This has immensely helped me in making quality decisions.

If you want to live a healthy and happy life, transforming your inspiration or knowledge into a daily habit is the way to go about it. Although cultivating good habits is one of the best ways to improve your experience, have you ever thought about why it is so important to eliminate bad ones? These are some reasons you need to develop good habits:

1. Your Habit Is Who You Are

Something you do every day without giving it a deep thought is called a habit. These routines ultimately become who you are. For instance, if you wake up every day to brush your teeth or maintaining a healthy lifestyle, it means you are someone who cares about your health. It might interest you to know that people can see a lot about you through the habits you practice, which will form the basis of their opinion about you.

2. Habits Can Work as a Source of Motivation

Of course, sometimes you won't feel like eating well, working, or exercising. However, transforming or developing these activities into habits will make them become your second nature, making you do them without even thinking twice.

It is worthy to note that having a solid foundation for healthy habits will immensely suit you for the rest of your life. It is not an impossible task to develop a healthy routine. And you can make the process easier for yourself with the proper practice and determination. It is not an impossible task.

3. Habits Set Your Foundation for Life

Either good or bad, the habit you decide to inculcate will ultimately set the tone or the foundation of your life. This is because your habit becomes you. You will end up becoming a joyful person if you have a habit of greeting your family with joy. You will become a healthy person if you have developed the habit of eating vegetables with each meal. By choosing to create good habits, you set yourself up to live a healthy and happy life.

4. You, Will, Reach Your Goals with Good Habits

You won't jump into the first marathon offered by your city without training if you have been dreaming about becoming a marathon runner. For you to even become fit and successfully take part in that marathon, it may take months, and sometimes years, of careful preparation. Get into the habit of looking for work every day to find a new job. Therefore, the first step to reaching your goal is to first establish a daily habit.

5. Your Habits Can Be Changed

Although it might be difficult, one of the best things is that we can change it. But you note that the worst the habit, the harder it is to stop. All you need to do is start skipping your morning scone until it becomes second nature to pass up the sugary pastries at breakfast if you want to eat healthier. If a habit once worked for you to achieve your goal, and it seems like it is no longer working, you can simply change it to another one.

6. By Making It Easier for You to Take Steps Toward Your Goals, Habits Can Help You Maintain Motivation

Habits allow you to change something significant that seems unachievable to something small or manageable so that you can do them each day. Commit to making five cold calls to potential new clients every day if you want to grow your business. If you want to write a book, you need to write at least 1,000 words a day. Commit to reading relevant news and articles for 30 minutes every day to build your expertise in a particular area.

What is success?

Have you ever asked yourself what you consider as success? Take some time to think about what metrics you count as part of being successful. Having millions or perhaps billions of dollars in the account? A happy family? Good health? Academic or professional success? A life without actual problems? Name it. It can be anything. As I mentioned earlier, success means different things to each one of us. All of us can't see from the same perspective. We come from different backgrounds, different races, different environments, and distinct realities. Therefore, our definition of success can never be the same. The same logic goes for failure. We all can't see loss from the same perspective because our realities and experiences are different.

So, the question to ask is: *"What does success mean to me?"* Since our definition of success varies, you should therefore be the one to set the standard of success for yourself and not what others define as success to you. What matters most is that whatever definition you consider as success, there is a goal in that direction. Now ask yourself: am I successful? If I am, what accomplishment am I proud of? If I am not, what is it I have to achieve to feel accomplished? Is there a successful person I look up to? Who is the person?

Ipsos surveyed on behalf of Strayers. They interviewed 2,011 Americans from age 18 upward, and they revealed that 67% of Americans consider success as being able to achieve personal goals; 66% believe a good relationship with family and friends as success, while 60% believe what they do for a living as success.

Is there something one could watch out for when identifying a successful person? Despite the subjective understanding of the term success, all the people who share this quality have some traits in common.

You should include these in your personality kits if you want to be successful.

Understand that these are not innate abilities, and if you don't have any of them, all you need to do is consistent with and integrate them into a part of your everyday life.

Here are some characteristics of a successful person:

1. Not Giving Up and Decisiveness

A strong will guarantee if back your path to success. You will inevitably have to decide if you want to stay on the way to success. Some will be hard; others will be easy; some will be wrong, while others will be right. But each one of them is necessary.

Your first instinct is usually to run when a hard time comes. This is because our brain is not comfortable with unpleasant situations. However, you will grow as a person and a leader if you can manage this period. Therefore, not throwing in the towel is a fundamental key to success. Do you want to be a successful entrepreneur? You need to look up successful entrepreneurs. Have a chat with them if you know anyone of them, and of course, they will always offer you an instrumental piece of advice.

2. Discipline

One of the most essential characteristics of a successful person is being disciplined. Without self-discipline, no hard work is efficient (or practical). Achieving success is a matter of hard work.

Having a schedule, timetable, or a plan in front of you allows every task—no matter how small — to have a sense of purpose. And when you can follow these steps, you are on your way to success. Have you noticed that self-disciplined people always have their eyes on their goals? They give time to plan their activities and also don't waste time. If you, therefore, want to be successful, imbibe the habit of the disciple in whatever you do.

3. Taking Risk

One thing you must have noticed about those who take risks is that they are always on the lookout for better opportunities.

In most cases, this idea often seems uncertain and unsafe.

However, it is sometimes necessary to take a leap of faith and dive into the unknown to succeed. Even when the odds seem uncertain, it is still not a solid reason not to give it a trial.

You are in if you have expert knowledge in such a field. And it is also acceptable to try it if you have enough trust in the surrounding people.

Taking a risk can be anything. It can be unexpectedly honest with someone you are close to and accept an unexpected job opportunity.

4. The drive to change

Someone with a strong will is always ready to grow personally or professionally. You must try as much as possible to gain new knowledge and new skills that will help you attain the position you want. Always be open to tasks you don't see coming, as they mostly come with an opportunity to grow. When you can manage problems relating to your field, you will gain new knowledge or learn a new skill and thrive in it.

5. Motivation and aspiration to succeed

You should have one or more goals you want to achieve at every moment in your life. This will give you a clear view of the future and keep you on your toes. Your motivation and aspirations serve as the checkpoint that will ultimately help you attain your goals.

I will advise you never to lose motivation. Try applying a slight change to your goals if you feel that your reason is melting away or your aspirations are fading.

You can do this by breaking your immediate goals into achievable, smaller steps or by switching the direction in which you are going at the moment.

Habit and Success

As mentioned earlier, changing habits is difficult because it complicated the neural pathway configured with those habits to replace. But the fact is, it is possible. Where there is a will, there is a way.

Now, the question: how is this connected to our everyday habits? Does habit play any role in expediting our attainment of success? How do our practices affect how success? The answers to these questions are what we would look at in this segment.

I must quickly mention that the impact our habits have on our success is highly significant. Your habit shapes your personality and your life, and they further shape and decide your accomplishments in life. Routines can help you determine and achieve your full potential and succeed in life, whether imposed by an external factor or by yourself or gained earlier or later in life.

I divided the nature of habitual activities into three parts: character, intellectual, and motor habits.

Motor habits are concerned with posture and movement, such as sitting, standing, exercising, and posture.

Intellectual habits are those concerned with the psychological process in the brain, reasoning, logical thinking, perception, observation, etc. The habit of character characterizes your behavior. Examples include: working hard or hardly working, polite communication, time management, cleaning the room/house, helping someone in need, etc.

Let us discuss examples of these traits and how they influence your success. You may adopt the following items to check your potential and decide on the habit include in your daily life.

Always Express Your Creativity

Innovative, imagine, creative people are those who succeed.

The world has changed and will continue to change. It is only the creative set of people that can adapt to it. Are you part of those people? And even if you are not, it is possible to become one.

It will make you happy if you do something for your enjoyment. Try writing. Try drawing or painting. It doesn't have to be a work of art. You don't have to show it to anyone. All that is required of you is just to enjoy the process.

You will free your mind from stress and worries when you engage yourself in creative works. This is the same benefit you gain when you do exercise, as it also prepares you for future mental strain and relieves you under pressure. Try it yourself if you don't believe it.

We are all creative in our way. If you have the habit of creating something, even if you throw it away right away after completing it, you will trigger unique processes in your brain. Who knows? These unique processes could help trigger an innovative idea.

Is Your Rapport Good with Other People?

It was Aristotle that said, *"Man is a social animal."* Yes, he is right. Without the help of other people, you can't achieve anything.

It is, therefore, crucial to maintain good relationships with people around you—both with familiar or unfamiliar faces.

It is easy as it seems. Think about it, whenever you go to the grocery store, do you smile at the cashier? Do you often say "please" and "thank you"? Such pleasantries are the foundation of good communication. Every other form of communication is built on it.

When you show interest in what people are telling you or the people talking to you, others will respect you because they will see that you are people.

You would be approached for collaboration.

No one wants to listen to someone always talking about themselves or someone frowning.

This is a habit, as well as a skill. You can incorporate it into your daily life. Remember that when you wait in an unending cash register, a *simple "enjoy the rest of your day"* to the cashier will brighten your day and theirs.

Denying Yourself a Break

Taking a pause is one of the most important habits that many people forget or ignore. All you need sometimes is just to relax and let go of everything. Sometimes, enough has to be enough.

Do you practice this? Do you always feel you should work instead of resting?

And when I mean rest, I mean ranging from a 2-week vacation in a 5-star hotel to a 5-minute break during your work rush.

We all need a break in our lives, and it is essential to identify when you need to step a little back from things when you have reached your limit. Just let go at that moment.

Spare some time to refresh, and you notice that your work will continue smoothly, with a re-energized strength.

Ensure that you start as soon as possible if you don't have this habit. We sure will.

Develop a never say never spirit

At the beginning of this book, I mentioned the characteristics of not giving up.

Of course, we can well consider this a habit. I used many people to always give up after their first failure.

Do you think you can achieve anything with such a habit if you give up too quickly?

If you have given up every time you failed at something, where would you be now? You are likely to still be at the very beginning of the road. Some people are less persistent, while some are more.

Every time you encounter a new challenge, it is good to always try as much as possible to push the limit a little further.

It won't hurt. Give it one more try! It could work out.

Be Self-discipline

It seems pretty easy to practice this habit. Simply make a to-do list, and ensure that you stick to it. You will be organized and having time for your activities.

Many people always wish to be successful in doing this, but are not. Are you part of such people? You must have your work well-planned if you want to be successful in something.

Practicing self-discipline is ought to unfold and business functions. When you start work, this can be learned, although it is problematic that way.

But without the pressure of a deadline or your boss, if you do this (more or less strictly) at home, that is when you display having the true potential to be successful in life.

Success comes from being organized. Nothing comes from being lazy, and you are presenting yourself as someone with whom others can be corporate and reliable.

Always try to improve yourself

You can grow in different ways. Achievement is only possible through self-growth. For instance, you can start taking classes and gain new skills. It is possible to read books in your area of interest. For an exciting opportunity, you can make yourself available. You become a better person with every new experience.

There is no how you will encounter a novel experience without it affecting your life; even though the experience doesn't seem better at first sight, but you can make it worthy.

Question yourself: *"What will I do for my growth today?" "Did I have a learning opportunity yesterday?"*

Never take this for granted. Even if it is something as simple as learning a keyboard shortcut today, you have become more knowledgeable.

Imagine this: if you learn a piece of new information each day for a year, it means you have discovered 365 unique pieces of information in a year. Therefore, the habit of constantly improving yourself is something you should integrate into your lifestyle.

Always set a goal

If you are at a point in your life where you are sure about what you want out of life, then congratulations. Not everybody does.

Smart people always have a goal they wish to attain. To add to that, the goal they are pursuing is not the only goal they are after, but similar smaller goals attached to the original purpose that will eventually lead them to the initial plan.

Another goal is set when one goal is achieved. You won't lack motivation in this way, and you will have a sense of achievement. If you don't have a plan you are striving to achieve, get one right now!

Don't fear dreaming big. Try as much as possible to think about the path that leads to your goal, and take it a step at a time, one small step followed by another.

By so doing, you will indeed develop a habit of setting goals for yourself, which will push you closer to your dreams.

Eat healthily

We all know the importance of food on physical wellbeing but may not know much about its impact on mental health. I don't want to bore you with research findings and statistics here.

I will just focus on why following a healthy diet is crucial to having a successful life.

To function correctly, you need to eat healthy foods.

If you combine good sleep and exercise, you will be a strong and healthy person. You may notice from the observation that when you skip any of these three, you are likely to become less productive, which will lower your chances of achieving your goals.

So, try putting these three items on your daily to-do list

Exercise regularly

We all need to constantly engage in exercise to keep fit. It is a mandatory part of everyone's life. Exercise helps with heart work and blood pressure normalization, muscle strength, and healthy weight.

But the focus of this section is the impact of exercise on the mind. You need to understand that engaging in physical activities helps to relieve anxiety, anger, stress, and negative energy. A person who doesn't work out may have difficulties lowering their stress level.

Exercise helps to calm you and reset your mind after a workout. It makes you be able to think more objectively and clearly.

Therefore, the question you need to ask yourself is that: *"do I exercise enough?"*

Do I sleep enough?

It is a fact that having a healthy sleep has many benefits. But what do you define as healthy sleep? It is important to note that this varies from one person to person. However, according to the scientist, healthy sleep should be on the average of 7-9 hours.

The health benefits of healthy sleep should be considered briefly. Healthy sleep helps to maintain weight. It lowers blood pressure. It improves your immune system and helps to regenerate your body.

There are other benefits of healthy sleep-related to brain function, as they contribute to what determines your chances of success. You will be in a better mood if you sleep well. If you sleep well, you will have a more substantial concentration power and the mental and physical strength to deal with work.

I will prepare your body to give effort and deal well with stress and strain if you get a healthy sleep every night.

Some examples of how habits have translated to success for some very successful people

- *Gary Vaynerchuk:* CEO Gary Vaynerchuk, VaynerMedia cofounder, a lifelong entrepreneur, and longtime tech investor, is undoubtedly one of the most successful people in the business tech industry. He has invested in over 50 startups, including Twitter, Tumblr, Medium, Birchbox, Uber, and Venmo. In an interview with the Insider, he shared his daily routines, which he has transformed into good habits to be more productive. His day starts immediately. He opens his eyes. Waking up early, reading the tech news, reading Twitter, workout, and meetings.

- *Jeff Bezos:* Jeff Bezos has a lot on his desk. Currently, he is the CEO of Amazon—an e-commerce landscape that operates a grocery store, developing A. I voice and producing movies. These are besides being the owner of Washington Post and the founder of Blue Origin. You would imagine his days to be so filled with so many activities. His days are usually not rushed. Instead, he allows himself to rest and recharge, making careful decisions. His typical days are sleeping and waking up early, reading the newspaper, having breakfast with kids, and starting the workday with the most critical meetings.

- ○ **Oprah Winfrey:** Only a few household names are as loved, respected, and trusted as Oprah Winfrey. She has had a substantial financial and cultural impact on the lifestyle of millions of people worldwide. Her typical day starts with exercise, eating vegetables, writing notes of gratitude, and spending the rest of the day keeping tabs on her finance.

I highlighted these examples to let you know that there is no successful person without a habit that has developed into a daily routine.

5 Ways to Make A Habit Stick

The year is gradually coming to a wrap. Seeing your enthusiasm for the new year, you notice it is fading because you have entertained excuses, and I have pushed your new year's resolutions to the back burner and overtook them. It is difficult to form and stick to a new habit initially, but they built big goals. These are few ways to make a habit stick if you feel your discipline is waning:

Take a baby step: start small

You will not climb Everest this weekend if you don't hike regularly. You need to break your goal down incrementally if you have a big plan, like running a marathon, getting a new job, or going to the gym five days a week. For instance, try running two miles a day, three days a week, and build on that if you want to run a marathon and you are not much of a runner. You will most likely fail and destroy your morale if you try to do too much at once. Build on your progress. Start small and have patience.

Know what your excuse is

What usually prevents you from practicing the habit? Do you forget to pack your lunch or forget your gym clothes? Is it because you are tired? Did you run out of time? Consider what is preventing your success in forming your habit. You can address them once you can pinpoint the excuse that prevents you from sticking to them.

Allow Your New Habits

You need to set yourself up for success. Start packing them the night before if you do not go to the gym. Pack it the night before if you forget to pack your lunch. If you don't take your commitment to go to the gym like an appointment, you will always find an excuse not to go by addressing your obstacles and usual excuses and preparing for success.

Failure is part of the process

At a point in our life, we would fail, which is very fine. Failure is part of life, and it is a growing process. Whether you cannot send a job application before the deadline, skip a workout, cheat on a diet, just ensure that you get back to it the following day. Success is not giving up despite failure and rejection, so do not lose heart whenever you experience a setback. Keep working.

Keep Track

Measuring your progress helps keep you motivated as you work towards your goals. Keep track of how many network connections you make and build on it and how many applications you send if you are trying to get a new job. What gets measured gets managed. Keeping track of your progress also helps to motivate you to stay consistent with your newly developed habit.

Celebrate little success

It is essential to have a mechanism in place that will help fuel your sense of accomplishment and motivate you in the long run. You will create those feel-good responses well before the actual habit is formed by celebrating tiny wins.

For instance, say something positive about yourself after making a healthier choice if you are starting a healthier lifestyle. Don't forget that the little things matter.

Reflection

➢ Look at your daily routine and determine which habits have proven beneficial to you and which have not.

➢ Try to see if you can do more of the helpful habits and less of the harmful ones.

➢ How would you define success?

➢ How do you measure your success?

➢ How do you make yourself successful?

Chapter 2: Habits Keeping You Habits Keeping You from Success

"The chains of habit are too weak to be felt until they are too strong to be broken,"–Samuel Johnson

Just as there are habits that push you closer to success, there are also habits that can prevent you from making headway in your endeavors. Here are examples of such habits:

1. Being engulfed by failure

Never allow failure to pull you back. There is no shame in failure. Instead, be proud that you have discovered another way of not do whatever you set out to do, and you've learned from it. Every successful person you see today has failed. Success comes with failure. Failure is part of success. The most crucial thing in failure is to learn your lessons and make better decisions next time.

2. Not being able to apologize for mistakes

Owning up to mistakes can be difficult. For some people, admitting that their fault can be difficult, as it will hit their ego. You will earn people's respect if you take responsibility for your mistakes. When you apologize to people, you will gain their trust. They will also respect you. When you know that something is wrong and apologize, it enables you to be honest and open to.

3. Not questioning

Some people don't enjoy asking questions. But those constantly asking questions about what is unclear will provide better insight into the world around them. You will also gather the information you need to make better decisions if you ask questions. No one knows everything. I found those who think they already know everything about constantly making mistakes. You will even be open to what other people will say if you have developed an inquisitive mind, and this will make you gain feedback and advice when you need it the most.

4. Not improving yourself

If you want to be successful, you need to commit yourself to lifelong learning. It is not a coincidence that successful people are voracious readers. You will gain more knowledge through reading. New things are happening every day worldwide, and they are being documented in a book. Imagine what you will miss out on if you stop reading? You will, of course, be uninformed. Besides that, reading exposes you to a different perspective and ideas from the world's brilliant minds. You should always seek deeper insight, no matter how successful you are. Knowledge allows you to dream bigger and helps to enrich your imagination.

5. Not being able to identify when to let go

For example, you have changed tactics, invested resources, tried various strategies, and poured in endless hours on a project. But it is a losing proposition no matter how hard you try. A time will come when you just have to let go. It is difficult for someone emotionally connected to just walk away from something you have spent resources with and to. Even a captain of a sinking ship must be able to identify when to grab the preserver. But when you know when to move on, it will give you the freedom to focus on other opportunities and enterprises.

6. Discarding the importance of persistence

For success, don't assume that talent outweighs persistence. Although skill helps, and you can continually cultivate and sharpen it. When things become difficult, perseverance is what will keep you going. When you can stick to your project, working through it painstakingly, success will come.

7. Not working with a budget

If you don't have a budget, it will seriously undermine your chances of success. Careless spending usually leads to financial recklessness. Something as small as paying attention to the most minor cost can add up. Having a budget can keep you on track financially if your impulsive or random purchases are sucking your budget dry. Finally, you will have less money anxieties if you stick with good money habits. It is therefore essential that you spend your time on some of that matter.

8. Always waiting for the perfect time

You may spend your life as a benchwarmer if you refuse to jump into the fray until it feels like the right time. It is one thing to take time to fine-tune your skills or taking calculated risks by watching the economy. But don't make fear prevent you from. You will never succeed if you never start.

9. Always wanting to be perfect

You will only set an unattainable bar for yourself if you are constantly striving for perfection. Because no one is perfect. You can be excellent at everything. As much as there are areas where you thrive, there are also areas where you will struggle.

You will fly times and falter another time. Accept that you will make mistakes instead of setting an unattainable expectation for yourself. You will grow stronger from your experience if you learn from your mistakes.

10. Comfortable in your comfort zone

Look at many business leaders who stepped out of their comfort zones, such as Warren Buffett, Larry Ellison, Richard Branson, and Bill Gates. You notice that at one point or the other in their lives; they failed. It is a scary proposition to take a risk. If none of them had taken risks, they wouldn't have been successful. Stepping out of your comfort zone means you are taking a leap of faith while also considering the possibility of failure. Unless you try, you may never know what your actual capacity is. Understand that there is a possibility of a reward that comes with risk.

11. Putting others (or yourself) down

You are only inviting negativity into your life if you constantly put others down or negative self-talk. You will hold yourself back if you continuously tell yourself that *"I can't do anything right," "I am stupid,"* and words of such. Similarly, you drag everyone down when you do it to others. Shut down your inner critics when you talk yourself down, or better still, try replacing them with positive affirmations. Only try to focus on the good things around you and always look for a way to bring yourself and everyone around you up.

12. Entertaining distraction

You may not escape from distractions. There is always a distraction waiting for you at every corner you walk to, and our gadgets make up the most prominent means. It is hard to focus your thoughts when your attention is scattered in a million directions. Your goals are being sidelined if you are living a distracted life. You are stifling your success if you continue feeding your distractions. Take a deep breath when you bounce from one task to another. Pause for a while, and calm your mind. Doing this will increase your productivity and help you concentrate.

13. Procrastination

You can't get anything done with procrastination. It is easy to get suckered into procrastination and complacency with so many distractions out there. It will lead to stagnation if you cannot keep. Indifference and inertia will eventually overtake you if you are afraid of taking the next step. You need to stop planning and start doing, at some point. A leader is someone who seizes opportunities and springs into action.

14. Self-doubt

Doubting yourself will facilitate the death of your dream. Your pessimistic feelings will become self-fulfilling if you constantly doubt yourself and question whether your goals are attainable. Fear of rejection or negative thinking of yourself will only fuel your indecisions and uncertainty. Please avoid negative thinking. If you are holding yourself back, you cannot succeed. You are much more likely to succeed if you believe in yourself and visualize your success.

15. Not paying attention to your health

Bad habits such as not getting enough sleep, not exercising, and eating poorly will leave you physically and mentally exhausted and potentially expose you to stress and illness. When you are prone to anxiety or disease, it will affect your ability to perform. You need to understand the importance of taking time to enjoy your life. You are probably missing out on everything else if you are busy working hard and taking life seriously.

16. Undefined goals

Many people have dreams, concepts, and ideas that they want to bring to life. But you have no way of achieving anything without a firm plan and clear vision. The first thing you need to attain your goal is to define it. This involves drawing a road map that will guide you to the destination. You can gallop off course without even knowing it if you don't have a plan to pull you into the future.

17. Always shifting the blame

No one enjoys taking blame. If given a chance, we would like to take any blame off our shoulders. It is even natural to want to attribute shortcomings to something else or someone. Start taking action instead of making excuses. Instead of shifting the blame, start considering the changes you will make to fix the problem. You have control over your step, no matter what the circumstances may be. Always turn your negativity into positivity.

18. Seeking approval

You are not listening to yourself if we focus you on what others think of you. You will only hold yourself back if you try to get approval from people. Of course, sometimes you will need other people's opinions, but you don't need constant accolades from people around you. Nobody is you. You are you with your failure and successes. You must eventually stand on your own.

Breaking Bad Habits

We all have habits, and there is nothing wrong with that. Some patterns are helpful. Maybe you like sorting out your clothes at night against the next workday, turning off the light before sleep. Or even something else.

But some other habits, such as hitting snooze too many times, drinking caffeine too late in the day, or biting your nails, might not be so beneficial.

It is difficult breaking unwanted habits, particularly if you have been engaging in them for so long. But having a grasp of how habits are formed is the first process.

How Habits are formed

Some theories have explained how habits are formed. One of the fundamental theories is the idea of the 3Rs:

➢ Reminder: This is a spark, cur, trigger that can be a conscious behavior such as nervousness, a feeling, flushing the toilet, or anything at all.

➢ Routine: we associate this with a trigger. Doing something repeatedly can make it become a routine. Feeling nervous triggers biting your nails while flushing the toilet cues you to wash your hands.

➢ Reward: The pleasurable release of dopamine in your brain can make you want to do it again if you do something that causes enjoyment or relieves. The compensation associated with a behavior allows the habit to stick.

Armed with the idea of 3Rs in mind, these are tips that will help up break a stubborn and old habit:

Know what triggers you

The first step to developing a habit is the trigger. The first thing you need to get past your bad habit is to identify your motivation. Track your practice to confirm if it has a pattern. Pay attention to things like:

> ➤ Does this happen immediately after something else?
> ➤ Is there anyone involved?
> ➤ How do I feel whenever it happens?
> ➤ At what time does it happen?
> ➤ Where does the habitual behavior happen?

Imagine that you want to cease staying late up at night. You will realize you stay up late if you chat and watching TV with friends after dinner. After a few days of tracking your behavior, you know you go to bed earlier after taking a walk or reading. Therefore, eliminating the trigger—chatting with friends, watching TV will make it difficult to carry out the routine of staying up late.

Pay attention to what you want to change

Is there a reason you want to change the habit? According to 2012 research from a source, it may be easier to change your behavior when the change you want to make is beneficial.

Take some time to think about why you want to change the behavior and the reward you gain from your habit change. Outlining these reasons may help you track a few that you haven't noticed occurred to you yet.

To motivate you more, you may choose to write your reasons in the bathroom, on your fridge, or somewhere you will see it regularly.

Pasting it where you can see it will make the change you are trying to effect fresh in your mind. Your list reminds you why you want to keep trying if you fall back into the habit.

Find a friend to support you

Try to do it together if you and a friend or partner want to break an unwanted habit.

For instance, you both want to quit smoking. I can think that dealing with this habit alone and leaving along with a friend won't make the cravings disappear. But when facing someone else, they might be easier to deal with.

Endeavor to always encourage each other through setbacks and cheer other's successes.

Even if they don't have any habits they want to change, a friend can still offer support. Try to open up to a trusted friend about the practice you are trying to break. If they notice you slipping back into old habits, they can gently remind you of your goals and encourage you in times of doubt.

Practice mindfulness

With mindfulness, you can develop actions, feelings, and awareness around your thoughts. This habit of practicing mindfulness involves observing impulses that connect to your routine without reacting or judging them.

You may find it easier to consider other options, such as not acting on the urges or avoiding reminders, as you become more aware of these routine behaviors and the triggers that lead to them.

When you practice mindfulness, you will note how your habits affect your daily life. You may feel more driven to change the pattern as you recognize how it affects you.

Get another habit to replace it with

Instead of just stopping the unwanted habit, if you replace the unwanted behavior with new behavior, you might have an easier time breaking the habit.

Imagine you don't want to keep reaching out for candy whenever you are hungry at work. You might fall back into the habits when you are hunger with a candy dish on your table.

The impulse to follow the new routine develops as you repeat the new behaviors. When you eventually see the rewards of the new habits—more minor sugar crashes and more energy—the urge to continue with the new behavior will be stronger than continuing with the old tradition.

It is beneficial when you replace harmful habits, such as substance abuse, with positive ones. However, you also remember that good habits, for example, exercising, can be excessive. Even healthy eating can have a negative effect when it's outrageous.

Find a way to constantly remind yourself

Use visual reminders, sticky notes, stickers, etc., wherever the habit happens, as it can help you rethink the action when triggered.

These are a few ideas you could consider:

> Leave a dish for your key. You will see it whenever you return home if you want to keep your keys in a designated area for you to stop losing them frequently.

> Leave a note for yourself on the light switch or door if you want to remember to turn off the morning when you leave a room.

> Try leaving small stickers on your refrigerator that you will see when you go to reach for a can if you want to break the habits of drinking soda with every meal.

A smartphone can also help you with a reminder. Set your alarm and write something motivational for yourself such *as "Remember how it feels when you take your after-dinner walk"* or *Time to switch off the TV.*

Change your environment

Your environment might have a substantial impact on your habits. For instance, you are trying to stop the habit of always wanting to order a takeaway because you spend too much on it. But you see the go-to menu hanging on your fridge every time you go into the kitchen. You could change the menu by changing the printouts of recipes you are sure you would enjoy.

Consider these examples too:

- ➤ Going to work through another route to avoid passing the café with an overpriced, tempting latte.

- ➤ Spending 15 to 20 minutes every evening arranging your house to encourage you to keep things clutter-free.

- ➤ Leaving hobby items, a journal (games, crafts, or sketchbook) on your coffee table gives you the motivation to pick them up as against scrolling through social media.

Also, note that the people that surround you are also part of your environment. It is advisable to take a break from those who don't support your process of breaking the habit.

Reflection:

- ➤ Review the habits listed in this chapter. Are you guilty of these?
  - ○ Ask yourself.
    - ■ What is this behavior really about?
    - ■ What do I want when I turn to this behavior?
- ➤ How else can I get what I want without turning into this habit?

Chapter 3: Characteristics of Successful People

"Success is walking from failure to failure with no loss of enthusiasm."–Winston Churchill.

In my course of the research, a unique aspect that consumed a chunk of my time is researching some characteristics of successful people. I investigated the factors of over 2,000 politicians, authors, celebrities, astronauts, and even CEOs. I always noticed some common traits when speaking to these individuals. These traits lead to their success. I could come up with a list of their characteristic. There are they:

1. **They don't just consume; they create:** The time when most people are listening to podcasts, radio, watching TV, reading emails, successful are busy coming up with ideas, creating new tools, coming up with

presentations, etc. Instead of being on the other end of the spectrum, consuming, they are the ones who are making things that people need.

2. **More than the payout, they are more excited about the journey:** When you walk or work with successful people, you will know they don't get involved in a get-rich scheme. They are more concerned about expressing their creativity, risk-taking, and are focused on building a sustainable career through hard work. Despite the obstacles, they enjoy the journey because they are busy doing something meaningful in their lives.

3. **They know their place in the world and who they are: You notice successful people are confident and lead themselves** and others well. They are dedicated to bringing their vision and mission to life every day. That is what they are always busy doing. Knowing who they are doesn't waste time on things that are not satisfying or something they are not good at.

4. **They are lifelong learners: they do not stop being learners once they graduate; most people believe that when they have graduated, they have finished** learning and studying. Successful people consider themselves a student for life, for they understand that learning is a continuum. Their habit of continuous learning enriches their experience and knowledge base. They are not scared of trying and failing in recent activities.

5. **They pitch the right questions to those who can deliver the correct answers:** It is common for successful people to tap into their network to ask the right questions to those who will have the correct answers. They are not scared of calling or emailing the best person who has answers to their questions. You will see them always prepared with the right questions, and they are always ready to help people.

6. **They can express their stories effectively:** they will tell you everything concisely if you walk up to a successful person and ask them what they do. You can believe in them. They know who they are and what they do. They are confident, persuasive, and have an assertive posture.

7. **Successful people will change to stay relevant in the business world.** If you ignore the trends, they will leave behind you. They are always coming up with new concepts and ideas, acquiring new skills, and always searching for the next big thing.

8. **The change doesn't affect them. Instead, they make changes:** successful people don't get affected by economic trends, but they are the ones who decide the direction and make things happen.

9. **They take responsibility for their actions and themselves:** they don't rely on others to get any job done. What they do most time is to look inwards and

seek solutions to their problem while leveraging on their current assets. They own up to their mistakes and immediately think of ways to improve next time if they make mistakes. They do this in order not to make the same mistake twice.

10. **It is common for successful people to already have their day planned out.** While unsuccessful people are scrambling to figure out what they need to do next, successful people wake up and have already planned their day. Their goals align with their strengths, focused, extensive, yet obtainable. They understand their weaknesses and know what they are capable of, and they are ready to invest as much time and resources into it to come to life.

11. **They understand they are in charge of their luck:** you will be lucky when you position yourself for success and have been hardworking. This is one characteristic you will find in successful people. You can't just randomly get lucky, and successful people understand that. What they do is to put themselves in the position of being fortunate by doing something every day that will push them to their luck, then use that luck to grow.

12. **They are ready to cannot succeed:** Successful people know that success is difficult and failure is a step towards success. They also know that they are bound to encounter more failure than success to succeed in anything. What differentiates them from unsuccessful

people is that they are ready to learn from their failure to make better decisions that will lead to success next time. Successful people will preserve when many people are giving up because of failure.

13. **They always offer more than what they are asked of:** For successful people, their job description is simply the beginning of what they can do to get the work going. They will always ask to take on more challenging projects after completing their mandatory tasks. Successful people are ready to take up tedious jobs that no one will do. And they enjoy doing it.

14. **They know when to leave and stay:** successful people know when to fold their company, start a company, or change employers. They have excellent intuition and are not scared of making a hard decision, irrespective of opposing forces.

.. Now to Personal Traits, You Must Cultivate to Be Successful

Self-esteem

"Believe in yourself! Have faith in your abilities! Without humble but reasonable confidence in your powers, you cannot be successful." Norman Vincent Peale.

The cornerstone of a healthy personality is self-esteem. Be comfortable in your skin. Your reputation with yourself is your self-esteem. You have talents that can help you succeed, and you are also unique. Writing the quality you admire is the key to self-esteem. Acknowledging your positive traits improves your self-esteem; it may be a discipline or what you have a passion for. Write all your successes to date, and keep track of them so that even when setbacks occur, you won't feel bad, making it reduce your self-esteem.

When you have documented your accomplishments, it enhances your self-esteem. Also, you need to note that comparing yourself to others is the actual hindrance to high self-esteem. Two people can't be alike. So, you can't be anyone else, no matter how much you try. You, therefore, have to be comfortable with who and what you are. You will do better at work and feel more positive about life when you have high self-esteem.

2. Positive Mental Attitude

"A pessimist sees the difficulty in every opportunity; the optimist sees the opportunity in every difficulty." Sir Winston Churchill.

You can't find a well-rounded, successful person who complains all the time and is equally harmful. Something familiar that you will find in all successful people is that they have a positive attitude. When things don't go their way, they don't complain, as they know that most items will take care of themselves in the long run. Thus, you must constantly train yourself to look for the brighter side of life. A great way to stay positive is being grateful for what you have while striving for more.

You will accomplish your daily tasks with even more vigor if you are optimistic about the day. Last but not least, a positive mental attitude will benefit your performance at home and at work. Nothing is important than your overall happiness and inner peace.

Personal Care

"Rest and self-care are so important. When you take time to replenish your spirit, it allows you to serve others from the overflow. You cannot serve from an empty vessel." Eleanor Brown.

Ask any successful person if they have time to take care of themselves, and they will tell you that personal care is one reason they are successful. They always find a way of balancing their work and personal life. You need to ensure that you are at your best most of the time to achieve all you want out of your life. You need the energy to move closer to your cherished dreams. Meditate, do yoga, and exercise. They are all helpful in improving your health. You also need to have an adequate sleep. Many people often neglect the importance of sufficient sleep in self-care.

Someone medically recommended it to have 7-8 hours of sleep a day if you want to be at your best. When you take some time off work, you will be more creative, plus research has revealed that people are more innovative, not at work, but during vacations or when they are relaxed.

Communication

"The most important thing in communication is hearing what isn't said." Peter Drucker.

I spent a more significant chunk of our waking time on communicating, both verbal and written. It is, thus, an important reason for us to be clear about what we share and the best mode of communication that is suitable for us. Becoming a better listener and understanding the other person's point of view is one way we can improve our communication skills. Clarity is the key to communicating effectively. In his book 7 habits of highly effective people, Stephen Covey said, *"Seek first to understand then be understood."* Keep reading; writing continues to improve communication skills. Ronald Reagan was known as a great communicator. Irrespective of which side of the political side you sway, you must admire his simple communication strategy. His answer to everything was always straightforward.

Prioritization

"One of the very worst uses of time is to do something very well that need not be done at all."

We all have so many things that need to be completed. However, we are in a fast-paced world, and we don't have the time to get through it. Therefore, being able to prioritize is the key to success. Of course, there will always be something to do, but the ability to prioritize the irrelevant from the relevant is a must-have skill if you want to be successful. This is how you will go about it: when you have a list of things to do, first attend to items that will have the most significant impact on your immediate boss, business sponsor, and your stakeholders. Understand that there will always be something left undone, and you have to learn to say no to things that will waste your time and activities that are not in tandem with your ambition.

You need to also learn to control your time by saying no in order not to over-commit yourself. A good example is Jack Welch. He knew GE would only take part in businesses to be the first or second in that market. This worked big for GE and is also what led to the closure of many business units.

Risk-Taking

"Only those who will risk going too far can find out how far one can go." — T. S. Eliot.

All the successful people you know today had taken a calculated risk to become what they are today. Taking a risk doesn't have to be skydiving or bungee jumping; in fact, it doesn't have to be physical. Taking risks can mean going with your intuition. It may mean taking up something everyone has refused, as it has the potential to propel your career or help to stand you apart.

Nothing is guaranteed in this life, apart from death. So, before you take that leap, analyze it carefully and see if you are ready to fail in it. Note that even though it is essential to take a risk, never use it to put your families in distress.

Curiosity

"Live as if you were to die tomorrow. Learn as if you were to live forever." Mahatma Gandhi.

The ability to keep learning something new in their field of concentration is a highly kept secret among most successful people. Curiosity is the hallmark of learning. An excellent example of someone who kept learning till he died is Peter Drucker, the father of modern management. Throughout his lifetime, he was always learning something new. It keeps our mind in shape when we know something new every day, as it gives us a sense of accomplishment when our time is used wisely. Learning has no end because the world does not stop moving.

Jony Ive of Apple is an excellent example of curiosity and creativity. There was a time I stumbled across how he masterminded the new Apple headquarters. Norman Foster was called a Poet, whose company Apple hired to build the office at the reported cost of $5 billion. In his WSJ piece WSJ article on Jony Ive, he said: *said 'Jony works tirelessly at the detail, developing, improving, refining. For me, that makes him a poet.'* Peter Drucker said, "**The only thing that will not be obsolete is learning new skills**."

Passion and Practice

*"The more you sweat in training, the less you bleed in combat."
Richard Marcinko.*

Passion powers every success engine. Looking at Tiger Woods and Roger Federer, you will understand the value of love. At the top of his career, having attained the zenith of sporting achievement, he changed the way he swings to get an extra edge. He did this after winning the master's tournament by a record of 12 strokes in 1997.

He asserted: *"You can have a wonderful week... even when your swing isn't sound. But can you still contend in tournaments with that swing when your timing isn't good? Will it hold up over a long period? The answer to these questions, with the swing I had, was no. And I wanted to change that."*

Resilience can be latent in you, and it is only passion that can ignite it. Tiger Woods played golf for the love he has for it. But the money also helps. When you do something you love and always give it your best, you have a passion for such things. Research had revealed that prodigies of The Beetles, Bill Gates, Woods, Mozart had practiced for 1000 hours before success finally crowned their effort. Not until he was 21 did Mozart not produce his first masterpiece, by which time he had put in over 1000 hours of effort. The formula I will recommend is Consistency+Time+Practice+Deliberate+Practice+Passion= success.

Robert Greene Bill Bradley documented in his remarkable book *Mastery* that he became great in basketball because of his outstanding commitment to practice than anyone else and passion. Said in another way, he was resilient. He mentioned he used to practice that after school; he practiced for three and a half hours, on Sunday, and eight hours every Saturday, and three hours during summer. He continued practicing beyond the feeling of pain and boredom.

Resilience

"Fall down seven times, Get up eight times."—Japanese Proverb.

Based on her groundbreaking studies, Angela Lee Duckworth of Pennsylvania contends that the single quality guarantees success. Napoleon Hill also noted that "Every adversity carries with it the seed of an equivalent benefit." For instance, when you are sick, it might allow you to reexamine what is important to you and how you can make changes. Of course, sometimes setbacks will occur, but it is essential to persevere and have patience.

Talent can't replace resilience and persistence. A classic example is Steve Jobs. He started another company, NeXT and bought Pixar after he was fired from the company he started. He then patiently waited for the second coming of Apple, and the rest becomes history, as they say. The lesson derived from this is that you can be down, but it doesn't mean you are out.

Belief

"Keep your dreams alive. Achieving anything requires faith and belief in yourself, vision, hard work, determination, and dedication. Remember, all things are possible for those who believe." Gail Devers.

In 2017, Roger Federer took home his eighth Wimbledon. It was a fantastic event, putting into consideration that a lot of critics have written him off. Here is what he said after his victory: *"I kept believing and dreaming."* When no one believes in you, the key is to believe in yourself. You can't achieve what you want if you listen to critics. Be relentless in your pursuit, and never pay attention to your critics.

Reflection:

➤ Think about the successful people that you idolize.

➤ What traits and characteristics do they have in common?

➤ Do you have any qualities in common with them?

➤ How can you channel these traits to help you achieve success?

Chapter 4: Secret 1- It All Starts in Your Mind

Failure is only postponed success as long as courage coaches ambition. The habit of persistence is the habit of victory.–Herbert Kaufman.

The Importance of Belief and Mindset on Success

T*here are times when you feel success has eluded you. It mostly happens when you think you are closer to achieving something, but failure seems to be the next thing. You need a change of mindset that will open your eye to opportunities and possibilities to succeed in any aspect of life. Remember that it will be challenging to get to your destination when you don't know where you are going. I will discuss how mindset helps to separate people from success and defeat.*

Fixed and Growth Mindset

A writer and psychologist from Stanford University, Carol Dweck, stated in the book entitled "Mindset" that there are two types of mindset—the growth and the fixed. Usually, depending on the circumstance, people have both attitudes. If you can grasp the concept behind the two perspectives, it will help you know if they equipped you with the right mind for success.

If you think talent is the key to success, you have a fixed mindset. Intelligence and talent are inherent to you. You, therefore, don't develop aptitude, but accept failure whenever you encounter a task that you feel is beyond your abilities.

When you have a growth mindset, you believe that through persistence and learning, growth can be achieved. You are one of those who sees intelligence and talent as the foundation of success. Armed with a developmental mindset, you will always want to improve your abilities through dedication and persistence. You are likely to view setbacks and obstacles as learning opportunities.

This means that if you seek to succeed or excel, building a growth mindset can be highly constructive. You will learn from your mistakes, believe that nothing is impossible, and learn to pick yourself up after stumbling.

Positive vs. Negative Attitude

Flashback to the last time you failed. Can you remember how you reacted? Whether you need a positive or negative attitude toward your predicament, this is precisely how mindset affects behavior.

If you have a positive body language towards failure, your perspective on life can be that of disappointments, losses, and hopelessness. A person with a negative mindset is quick to feel victimized or defeated for your situation when dealt with difficulty or obstacle.

Conversely, having a positive attitude towards your challenges will help you overcome them more accessible. You are likely to see failure as a stepping stone that will lead you to the path of success.

Result of Changing your Mindset

By changing your attitude and transforming your perspective, a change in mindset affects your success. This will give you the confidence to pursue your new ideas. This will spark your motivation and help push you to win. Open yourself up to changes and be flexible. It will affect your relationship and impact your work.

Why you need to master your mindset for success

One of the most critical factors that will affect a person's level of success — whether in the personal or professional area of someone's life. What you think about always has a substantial impact on your behaviors and not the other way around. It is therefore vital to get this fundamental principle right.

A distinctive difference between those who succeed and those who don't be the mindset. And you must learn to master yours if you are serious about achieving success in any area of your life.

These are five reasons you need to master yourself:

1. Achieving the underlying goal

Setting your goals is multi-faceted. You may not get far without the proper mindset. Achieving a goal requires more than just a lukewarm desire to succeed, as success can easily elude even the most well-intentioned individuals.

Whether someone will dig deep and work through hardship to succeed or simply admit defeat, mental toughness determines that. Mindset is where the rubber meets the road. Before ultimately accomplishing the underlying goal, it includes leveraging self-talk to move through each pivotal phase, sustaining effort over long periods, and exercising courage.

If you are ready to command your desired result, you need to make a conscious decision to master your mindset and reach for more success in the days to come.

2. Facing Adversities

The path to your success is bound to include some adversity, no matter what goal you seek to achieve. However, you will need to learn to face each challenge and develop a thick skin if you want to get through the rough patches.

Mindset plays a crucial role during adversities. Troubles test your mettle. A person may feel justified in succumbing to defeat after facing extreme hardship. It strengthened resilient people to stay encouraged during adversities. Yet the capacity to get knocked down, and not knocked out, to move through the fire, is a wonderful power of a resilient mindset.

3. Harnessing Drive

Drive, as it implies, means to move from one position to another. Also, the unwavering determination to achieve an important aim is driving. The drive includes engaging in sustained effort over time and developing a vision for success. Achieving most goals would be difficult without purpose.

It can quickly urge someone to push comfort zone and challenge the status quo with the power to direct focus and encourage commitment to a higher purpose. The importance of the drive to mindset can't be questioned. Those with drive strive to accomplish more and are self-motivated. They don't waste time rambling about circumstances, but they often look at how to improve them.

4. Formulating a winning perspective

There are few things more valuable than perspective for success. The way we attach meaning to circumstances and events dramatically affects how you see the glass half empty or half full. "Nothing in life has any meaning except the meaning [we] give it." I credit this viewpoint to Tony Robbins. The thing you must note is that mindset has everything to do with perspective. Your attitudes, foundational beliefs, and biases affect the way and speed with which you process information and how you experience the world around you. Having an optimistic mindset increases your chances of achieving long-term success and planning a winning perspective.

5. Developing healthy self-esteem

A person must first feel capable of achieving a worthwhile feat to accomplish it. Whatever anyone thinks does not matter. Positively or negatively, self-esteem is derived from our internal dialogue that informs how we evaluate our worth. This is also what forms the concept or view we have about ourselves. It is no doubt that a positive and strong mindset is essential to developing healthy self-esteem. It is a crucial tool that affects our attitudes and feelings, reinforces our most personal beliefs and daily self-dialogue. So, plant the seeds of positivity and inspiration, and become the gatekeeper of your mind, rather than criticism and doubt.

Growth mindset habits for success

As mentioned earlier, a growth mindset believes that ability or skill can be developed and that a conscious effort to establish them means you have a growth mindset. A fixed mindset thrives on the belief that our abilities are fixed regardless of effort.

It is possible to have a fixed mindset towards life and a growth mindset in others. Practice cultivating these habits for a growth mindset if you recognize a fixed mindset in your life and transform it into one of growth.

1. Be open to new experiences and information

You will block your chance of learning if you have a fixed mindset. The world leader in growth mindset theory, Carol Dweck, conducted an experiment. He asked people with both growth and fixed mindset some set of complex questions. He then investigated their level of brain activities while giving their feedback on whether their answers were correct or wrong. From Dweck's experiment, he noticed that those with fixed mindsets only showed interest if they were told they had answered the question correctly. Their brain activity dialed down when information about answers they got wrong is provided. Those with a fixed mindset are, as a result, not open to learning new things.

Those with a growth mindset sustained a high level of brain activity when they were given feedback on their wrong answers, and the subsequent test showed that they had learned something new compared to those with a fixed mindset. So, what is the essence of Dweck's research? The research reveals to us the importance of maintaining openness to new information and experience. When we do so, our neurons wire and fire together, making our abilities and skills develop, bringing about a growth mindset.

2. Failure should not be viewed as all defining

This concept has been mentioned many times in this book. And it goes to show the importance of maintaining a positive attitude towards failure.

Rather than regarding failure as being all defining, avoid the fixed mindset trap by learning to view failure as a temporary setback. Even people with a growth mindset still experience disappointment and failure, but they don't allow it to drag them back and prevent them from achieving their goals. Next time, focus on what you can do differently and take a growth mindset approach to improve performance when things don't go as planned.

3. Celebrate your success

If you don't believe in your ability, you may not fulfill your full potential, persevere, or try new things. Make time to acknowledge and celebrate your success. Recognize how your hard work allows you to excel in an existing area of interest. Remember previous achievements that involved the learning process when you embarked on a new learning process and remind yourself that having a growth mindset made you achieve success.

4. **Be ready to take new challenges**

The idea of opening oneself up to new challenges has also been mentioned in this book. Accept it if it present again you with a task that you could not master in the past. Take it on again. By so doing, you will develop your abilities and skills, as you can only find growth outside your comfort zone. Dr. Hary Chugani, the neurologist, describes the complex connections in the brain during the learning process as having a similitude to roads. Chugani clarifies, *"Roads with the most traffic get widened. The ones that are rarely used fall into disrepair."* With practice, both with strength and improving your performance, new or challenging tasks are an opportunity to develop new skills and synaptic connections.

5. **Consider the impact of your words**

You need to ask yourself what impact do your comments have on the surrounding people? Do you encourage others to learn, develop and grow, and do you adopt a growth mindset? If not, you need to consider ways to improve your interaction with everyone for you to cultivate a growth mindset.

6. **Always look forward to a positive outcome**

The most famous willpower study creator, the marshmallow, psychologist Walter Mischel, contends that focusing on the positive outcomes when trying to reach their goal is essential for success. Try as much as possible to develop a vivid and clear picture of what your success will look like. Picture how you will feel when you have mastered a subject or skill and fix your mind on your desired outcome.

7. Don't allow negativity to affect you

Guard against being demotivated or being sidetracked by negative comments when you commit to change old habits. Of course, constructive criticism is essential, but paying attention to your inner voice, mindset, and growth is equally important. Separate the feedback you receive from people and yourself, and see a fixed or growth mindset inspire which ones. If a friend or a colleague were embarking on a new learning experience, consider how you would encourage a friend and coach yourself in the same way.

What is unsaid about success that will enable you to achieve your goals

    1. Focus on the process, not the results

You must have heard somewhere that success shouldn't be what you should aim for, but something else. We all focus on the success we want, such as becoming more positive, more fulfilled, healthier, building a business, etc., and these are important.

Let me tell you that the real value is not the outcome, as that is not where the growth lies. The work will only make us happy for so long. Here is it: we dampen our efforts and become trapped in a fixed mindset of failing or succeeding by focusing on the result. It prepares you for a rollercoaster ride of difficulties.

The world's top performers have realized that it is more important to focus on the repetition and quantity, not the outcome. Making 100 cold calls every day to your target customer is preferable to the perfect pitch. Writing a single book a year is more critical than the best-selling book.

How to apply it

Focus on improving the process that creates those outcomes instead of crafting the perfect result or habit. For instance, focus on improving your techniques and skills every day to become a great midfielder in soccer. Focus on creating the small viable product and selling to 1,000 customers first if you want to launch an acclaimed business, as against trying to craft a faultless product no one needs.

2. Work less, but do more

The quote simply explains that many people spend their energy on unimportant, small things and don't spend most of their energy on actions that will make a significant difference. Ask yourself which actions will offer the biggest impact on your goals if you want to understand this concept.

How to apply it

All actions are not equal. Check where you spend most of your time, and what you are doing to achieve your goals. For example, what is the number one habit that has the most significant impact on your success if you try to get toned or leaned? What simple thing can you do that has the most tremendous success if you build a positive culture?

3. Play hard to work hard

It takes long hours of long periods to achieve something you want, plus you have to work hard to achieve things in life. But don't you think it's cool to play and have fun as you did as a kid? Before, I used to believe that I significantly needed to work hard to achieve success. While that might be true, excessively working hard can create resistance, as my to-do list is always filled up. The mere thought of think about work drains me, let alone doing it. This made me do what many people did: delay, procrastinate, and avoid. I later learned this secret: what will happen if I replace *"work"* with *"play"*? It should seem fun; perhaps I will feel like someone who is on an adventure.

How to apply it

Is there a part of your life that is complex and mentally tiring? Is there a way to change your approach to work to make it fun and exciting for yourself? For instance, how can you make it more fun if you want to build productive habits? Can you treat it like art in class? Can you use crayons and glitter?

4. Know the importance of benevolence

You can be more successful by contributing to the world meaningfully. Not only that, but it can also make others successful. This is one of the nonlocalized secrets of success. As we all know, our existence is limited and fragile. We don't know how much time each one of us has left. We should therefore start asking ourselves what matters to us? What would we leave behind? And what purpose does the money you are making serve beyond paying the bills?

How to apply it

Take a sheet of paper and list causes you care about or are interested in. Go online and research people to support or find some organizations. You can contribute by sharing your expertise, skills, and becoming an advisor. For instance, I care about access to quality education for children in Africa. So, I help my organization connect sponsors and indigent but bright students so that the sponsor can take care of such child's education. The donation of the sponsor or donor can even come as donating a library or books to indigent communities. At the end of it all, I am always fulfilled that I have helped the children to gain access to education, giving them a shot to an opportunity for a quality life.

Reflection

➤ Think of something you are afraid of doing or are bad at. For example, if you're fearful of public speaking, focus on how you can improve rather than be perfect at it.

➤ What can you learn? Who from?

➤ What are you passionate about?

➤ What are you willing to give back to society?

Chapter 5: Secret 2- Know Where You Are Going

"People with goals succeed because they know where they're going."–Earl Nightingale.

The Importance of Goals

A re you used to setting goals? Do you ever revisit your goal list?

The importance of setting goals is not alien to us, as we all know its importance. As we move on through life, we often lose its significance and even place less credence in it. And one reason for such is because we find it boring and not engaging enough to make us feel enthusiastic about sticking to it. However, goal setting doesn't have to be boring. There are scores of advantages and benefits of creating, setting our goals, and working towards them.

Besides other advantages of setting goals, it helps you sustain that momentum in life, guide your focus, and trigger new behaviors.

When you have a goal you are trying to achieve, it promotes a sense of self-mastery and aligns your focus. In the end, you can't improve upon something that you can't manage. By setting your goals, you will do these and more.

In the subsequent pages, I will touch on the importance and value of goal setting and the many benefits.

I will also alight how goal setting can lead to outstanding performances and success. Besides motivating us, goal setting helps improve our professional and personal development and mental health.

The Value and Importance of Goal Setting

Goals were divided into three groups or types, not until 2001 (Elliot & McGregor, 2001):

1. Performance-avoidance goals
2. Performance-approach goals
3. Mastery goals

A performance-avoidance goal is one group that describes an individual who avoids doing the worse of their peer to prevent negative feedback

A performance-approach goal is an approach when an individual tries to do better than their peers. Such goals are something like getting a performance review or losing 10 pounds.

A mastery goal is a situation where individual sets to master or accomplish something such as *"I will score higher in my next exam."*

The research carried out by McGregor and Elliot in 2001 introduced a new perspective. It was assumed that mastery goals were the best, and performance-avoidance goals were deemed the worst, while performance-approach goals were sometimes good and evil, until this study was published.

As a result, the implied assumption was that there were no mastery-avoidance goals or wrong mastery goals. McGregor and Elliot's research challenged these assumptions by proving that each type of goal can be helpful depending on the circumstance and proving that master-avoidance goals do not exist.

McGregor's and Elliot's study used a 2 × 2 achievement goal, which entails:

1. Performance-avoidance
2. Performance-approach
3. Mastery-avoidance
4. Mastery-approach

Why do we set goals?

The fact is that some goals are achieved while some are not, and it is crucial to know why.

The author of the book *"Hard Goals: The Secret to Getting from Where You Are to Where You Want to Be,"* Mark Murphy, the founder, and CEO of LeadershipIQ.com, has extensively studied how the brain functions and how we are wired as human beings concerning goal setting.

Murphy's book combines exciting research and the law of attraction to help the reader fine-tune the process.

According to Murphy (2010), A HARD goal is an achieved goal. Murphy recommends we put our future benefit into the present and our present cost into the future. What this means is not to push what you could do today till tomorrow. We value things more in this present moment than we will do in the future time.

Setting goals changes. The goals you put into your teenage year will probably change in your adulthood. As long as you continually revisit your life goals and work on updating them, whatever your age doesn't matter in the end.

What is the importance of goal setting?

In the goal-setting theory, the likes of Gary Latham and Edward Locke are leaders. Goals affect behavior and job performance, but it also helps to garner energy that contributes to higher power overall. The higher effort brings about a continuous increase in persistent effort.

Factors such as ability and self-efficacy may affect, according to Lunenburg (2011), the motivational impact.

According to the research (Locke & Latham 1991), goal setting can be an effective technique under the right conditions.

If the goal is not accomplished, accomplishing the plan can lead to frustration and lower motivation or satisfaction, and further motivation.

Goals help motivate us to develop strategies that will allow us to perform at an optimal level.

How to Set a Goal

To achieve a goal, you first need to know what you would like to achieve and then commit to it. Set SMART (Specific, Measurable, Attainable, Relevant, and combined) goals. Endeavor to write them down. Then brainstorm steps you will have to take to achieve them.

The following suggestions will help you set practical goals:

Set realistic goals: You don't want to set a goal you can't achieve. Your environment or people around you can set unrealistic goals, such as the media, parent, employer, or even society. This is mainly done in ignorance of your ambitions and desires. So, whatever goal you intend to achieve, ensure that it is realistic and what you want, and not what others want for you.

Develop performance goals, not outcome goals: it's dispiriting to not achieve personal goals beyond our control. You should, therefore, only endeavor to set goals that you have control over. It could be just plain bad luck, injury, bad weather, or poor judging in sport. In business, the reasons could be unexpected government policy, lousy business environment, etc.

You can keep control over the achievement of your goals and draw satisfaction from them if you base your destination on personal performance.

Keep operational goals small: The low-level goals you are working towards should be achievable and small. It can seem that you are not making progress if it's too large. Keeping the goals paltry offers opportunities for reward.

Write down your goals: Writing your plan gives it force and crystalizes it.

Have a priority: Give your most important goal a priority when you have several purposes. This helps to direct your attention to the important ones and helps you avoid feeling overwhelmed by having too many goals.

Be precise: To measure your achievement, you need to set specific goals and put dates to them. You will know precisely when you have achieved a dream if you do this, which will make you more satisfied.

Put your goals in a positive statement: Put your goals on favorable terms. *"Don't make this stupid mistake"* is a negative term, but *"execute this technique well."*

Setting a lifetime goal

You need to consider what you want to achieve in your lifetime to set a personal goal. When you select a lifetime goal, you will have an overall perspective that shapes all aspects of your life's decision.

Try to set goals in some of the following categories to give a broad, balanced coverage of all critical areas in your life or in places where you feel it's essential.

> ➢ Public Service: Am I interested in making the world a better place? If so, then how?

> ➢ Pleasure: Do I want to enjoy myself? (I need to ensure that some parts of my life are for me)

> ➢ Physical: Do I want to achieve any athletic goals, or do I just want to keep fit until I am old? What step am I going to take to accomplish that?

> ➢ Attitude: Do I behave in any way that upsets me? Or is there any part of my attitude holding me back? (If so, I need to set a goal to help me find a solution to my problem and improve my behavior).

➢ Artistic: Is there any creative goal I would like to achieve?

➢ Family: Am I ready to be a parent? If so, how can I be a good parent? How do I want to be seen by my spouse and extended family?

➢ Education: What knowledge and skill will I need to gain to achieve my goals?

➢ Financial: What should be my average income, and at what stage? Is it related to my career goal?

➢ Career: what level do I want to attain in my career? What do I need to get there?

Examples of People Famous People Who Set Goals and Achieve Them

You may have come across different stories of how successful people set their goals and achieve them in their personal and professional life. But do you know how these people do it?

However, in the following pages, I will share how famous successful people can set their goals and change their lives from zero to hero.

Yes, many other people set goals and could achieve them, but I find the story of these few people quite inspiring, and besides, irrespective of the industry you belong, these people are big shots, and you must have heard about them at one point or the other.

So, let us quickly meet these people and discover how they can achieve their life goals.

1. Tony Robbins

He wrote his goals on an old Russian Map

Tony Robbins is one of the most prominent personalities in the personal development industry. He has transformed the lives of many people and continues to do so. Many people consider him the number 1 success coach, as he has coached the likes of Hugh Jackman, Nelson Mandela, Serena Williams, Leonardo DiCaprio, and Bill Clinton, just to name a few.

Just like most grass to grace stories, Tony Robbins started from rock bottom. In his best-selling book, Awaken the Giant Within, he shared how he wrote his goals on an old Russian Map. Let see what he wrote in the book.

Eight years ago, in 1983, I did an exercise that created a future so compelling that my whole life changed. As pan of the overall process of raising my standards, I established an entirely new set of goals, writing all the things I would no longer settle for and what it committed me to having in my life. I set aside all my limiting beliefs and sat down on the beach with my journal. I wrote continuously for three hours, brainstorming every possibility of what I could ever imagine doing, being, having, creating, experiencing, or contributing. The timeline I gave myself for achieving these goals was from tomorrow to the next twenty years. I never stopped to think whether I could achieve these goals. I simply captured any possibility that inspired me and wrote it down.

From that beginning, I refined the process six months later when I was invited, along with a group of parapsychologists, to the USSR to study psychic phenomena directly from university experts throughout Russia. As my group traveled the country, I spent many hours on the train from Moscow to Siberia and Leningrad. With nothing to write on but the back of an old Russian map, I wrote all my long-term goals for my spiritual, mental, emotional, physical, and financial destinies and then created a series of milestones for each one, working backward. For example, to achieve my top spiritual goal ten years from now, what kind of person would I have to be, and what things would I need to accomplish by nine years from now, eight years, seven years, and so on, reaching all the way back until today? What specific action could I take today that would lead me on that road to the destiny of my choice?

On that day, I set specific goals that transformed my life. I described the woman of my dreams, detailing what she would be like mentally, emotionally, physically, spiritually. I explained what my kids would be like, the vast income that I would enjoy, and the home that I would live in, including the third-story circular office area that would overlook the ocean.

A year and a half later. Life magazine was in my home, interviewing me about how I had made such incredible shifts in my life. When I pulled out my map to show them all the goals I had written, it was amazing to see how many I'd achieved. I had met the woman I described and married her. I had found and purchased the home I'd envisioned, down to the finest detail, including the third-story office in the castle's turret, overlooking the ocean. When I wrote them down initially, I had no assurances that these goals could be achieved. But I had been willing to suspend judgment for a short period to make it work.

That was how Tony Robbins set his goals. He practically sketched his future, envisioning it, as he knows what he wants to achieve, and put it down on a Russian map. So, have you written your goal yet?

1. **Scott Adams Wrote His Affirmation 15 Times every day**

It is possible not to have heard about Scott Adams. But if I ask if you've listened to Dilbert, you probably would have.

Scott Adams is one of the most successful cartoonists of our time, and he is the creator of the Dilbert comic. Dilbert has been written into hundreds of merchandised toys and games, animated series, successful best-selling books. It has also been published and syndicated into thousands of newspapers.

Like every other person, Scott Adams also started from scratch. He was a regular employee of 9-5. But he has always nurtured the dream of becoming a successful cartoonist.

One day, one of his friends shared how writing his goals 15 times every day can help him achieve his goal. He tried it. He stayed consistent with it, and the rest, as they say, is history.

These are the affirmations he writes 15 times every day

"I, Scott Adams, will become rich."

He bought two stocks, which ended up giving him a ridiculous win. He then sold the two stocks that gave him a considerable fortune. In his book How to Fail at Almost Everything and Still Win Big, he shared this story.

It worked. He then changed his affirmation and wrote this down 15 times a day:

"I, Scott Adams, will score in the 94th percentile on the GMAT."

In the coming weeks, Adams both GMAT study packs and practiced as much as possible. But each day, he scored 77th percentile. But he continues with his repetition of writing his affirmation 15 times every day.

He finally took the GMAT test, and the result came out. He had precisely 94th percentile. Of course, he believed in his affirmation technique.

Every morning before going to work, after earning his MBA, he would write this phrase 15 times

"I, Scott Adams, will become a syndicated cartoonist."

He became one. Not only that, he became one of the most successful syndicated cartoonists. According to an article, this was what happened next:

"Despite several setbacks and rejections, and through a series of unlikely coincidences and lucky breaks, he eventually became a syndicated cartoonist. In fact, he's arguably the most syndicated cartoonist alive today: Dilbert is published in 2,000 newspapers worldwide, in 65 countries and 25 languages."

This was how Scott Adams's repetition techniques translated into his achieved goals.

2. **Jack Canfield pictured making his first million**

Another inspirational figure I learned from Jack Carnified. I usually enjoy his styles and teaching methods. He is the world-renowned author for Chicken Soup for the Soul Series, which has over 250 titles and 500 million copies printed in over 40 languages. He is equally an entrepreneur, trainer, and motivational speaker.

The Success Principle is one of his books that I enjoyed reading and one of my top 10 all-time success books. You may check it out if you haven't.

So how did Carnified set his goals? And became successful? This was what he said:

"I've been using vision boards in one form or another since the 1970s. My first,"vision board was a $100,000 bill that I made myself.

I taped it to the ceiling above my bed to see it every day when I woke up. I set the goal for myself that I wanted to make $100,000 in one year. At that point, I was making $8,000 a year, so this was over 12 times my annual income.

Every morning when I would wake up, I would visualize that. I would close my eyes and imagine my $100,000 lifestyle.

What it would be like...

Where I would live...

The Navajo rugs I was going to buy I put on my walls...

The little lake house I would have...

The car I would own...

And everything else I could think of.

Guess what happened? Within about 30 days, I started having hundred-thousand-dollar ideas for the first time in my life.

Within a year, I had earned $92,000. It was a fantastic breakthrough.

At the end of that year, my wife asked me, "Do you think it'll work for a million dollars?" I said, "I don't know, it worked for $100,000. So, let's do it."

We made a million-dollar bill and put that on the ceiling. And within a few years, I received my first $1,000,000 check for a book royalty for the first Chicken Soup for the Soul."

Great, isn't it?

Jack Canfield employed the power of visualization to help his goals, just like how John Assaraf did it, which you will later get to know.

3. Bruce Lee became a Hollywood star after writing a letter to himself

One of the biggest Hollywood stars of all time is Bruce Lee. He was named one of the greatest heroes and icons and one of the 100 most essential people of the Century. Besides that, he has received stars as the founder of Jeet Kune Do, Hollywood Walk of Fame, and also as a philosopher, with different sayings credited to him, such as.

If you love life, don't waste time, for time is what life is made up of. — BRUCE LEE

You will want to ask: how did Bruce Lee rose to become a superstar in the movie industry, as well as a successful martial artist? Bruce Lee knew what he wanted; what did he do? He wrote his goals as a letter to himself. You will see a framed letter where Bruce Lee wrote to himself if you visit Planet Hollywood. Here:

My Definite Chief Aim

"I, Bruce Lee, will be the first highest-paid Oriental superstar in the United States. In return, I will give the most exciting performances and provide the best of quality in the capacity of an actor. Starting in 1970, I will achieve world fame, and from then onward till the end of 1980, I will have in my possession $10,000,000. I will live the way I please and achieve inner harmony and happiness.

Bruce Lee

As a promise and a commitment to meet the goals he set for his life, Lee wrote this letter on the 9th of January, 1970.

Unfortunately, he could not complete his goals because of his untimely death. However, I dare say that he has successfully reached his goal beyond his wildest dreams if you look at his achievements and what he has accomplished.

Now my questions to you: Do you see yourself writing a letter to yourself, promising to give what it takes to achieve all that you have written? Are you ready to be as committed as Bruce

Lee? If you are prepared to, then congratulations in advance. Bruce Lee did it, and he could reach his goals and became very successful.

4. John Assaraf vision boards that came to live

I was amazed and enthusiastic about creating my vision board when I first read about John's story of using his vision board to bring his goals to life. I read John Assaraf's book a lot and went through his training. In fact, he is my mentor.

John was one guru in the Law of Attraction industry. He featured in books like The Success Principles written by Jack Canfield. John was equally a New York Times best-selling author.

Do you want to know how he did it? This was how it began:

"In 1995, John Assaraf created a vision board and put it up on the wall in his home office.

Whenever he saw a materialistic thing he wanted or a trip he wanted to take, he'd get a photo of it and glue it to the board. Then he'd see himself already enjoying the object of his desire.

In May 2000, having just moved into his new home in Southern California a few weeks earlier, he was sitting in his office at 7:30 AM when his 5-year-old son Keenan came in and sat on a couple of boxes that had been in storage 4 years.

Keenan asked his father what was in the boxes. When John told him his vision boards were in the boxes, Keenan replied, "Your vision, what?"

John opened one box to show Keenan a vision board.

John smiled as he looked at the first board and saw pictures of a Mercedes sports car, a watch, and some other items, all of which he had gained by then.

But as he pulled out the second board, he cried.

On that board was a picture of the house he had just bought and was living in!

Not a house like it, but the house!

The 7,000-square-foot house that sits on 6 acres of spectacular views, with a 3,000-square-foot guest house and office complex, a tennis court, and 320 orange trees—that same home was a home he had seen in a picture that he had cut out of Dream Homes magazine 4 years earlier!"

5. **Jim Carry wrote a twenty-million dollars cheque to himself as his goal, and he could achieve it**

Jim Carry also has a grass to grace story. He was born into a poor family that lived in a Volkswagen van. But Jim knew his calling was more significant than that. In 1990, as a struggling young comic in Los Angeles, he drove his ancient Toyota to the top hill.

He sat there for a while, thinking about how he was going to live his future. He then wrote a $10 million check to himself and put in the notion line *"for acting services rendered."* The check had the date of 1995 fixed by him. It started when he put the statement in his wallet.

By 1995, Jim recorded tremendous success in The Mask and my favorite, Pet Detective, Ace Ventura, Liar, Liar. And his per film fee at that point had increased to $20 million.

6. **Tracy changed his life by writing his goals**

Brian Tracy is also an example of successful people who wrote their goals and achieved them. Brian Tracy is a self-development author of over seventy books translated into different languages and a motivational speaker.

In his book How to Get Everything You Want—Faster Than You Ever Thought Possible, he shared how he wrote his goals and achieved them.

The Day My Life Changed

Then one day, I took out a piece of paper and wrote an outrageous goal for myself. It was to earn $1,000 per month in door-to-door and office-to-office selling. I folded up the piece of paper, put it away, and never found it again.

But 30 days later, my entire life had changed. During that time, I discovered a technique for closing sales that tripled my income from the very first day. Meanwhile, the owner of my company sold out to an entrepreneur who had just moved into town. Exactly thirty days after I had written my goal, he took me aside and offered me $1,000 per month to head up the sales force and teach the other people what I did that enabled me to be selling so much more than anyone else. I accepted his offer, and from that day forward, my life was never the same.

Within eighteen months, I had moved from that job to another, and then to another. I went from personal selling to becoming a sales manager with people selling for me. I recruited and built a 95-person sales force. I went literally from worrying about my next meal to walking around with a pocket full of 20 dollar bills.

Within eighteen months, I had moved from that job to another, and then to another. I went from personal selling to becoming a sales manager with people selling for me. I recruited and built a 95 person sales force. I went literally from worrying about my next meal to walking around with a pocket full of 20 dollar bills."

This goes to show that goals work. Tracy got serious about the process after seeing the incredible results from writing his goals. That's how he became very successful.

Reflection:

➢ Think about how you want your life to be in 5, 10, 15 years

➢ Envision the different aspects of your life.—where do you live? Who are you living with? What occupies most of your waking hours?

➢ How different is that life from the life you're living now?

➢ What things make you happiest?

➢ How can you share your knowledge and experience?

➢ Who can help you achieve your goals?

➢ What would you like to be your legacy?

Chapter 6: Secret 3– Consistency, Consistency, Consistency

"We are what we repeatedly do. Excellence, then, is not an act but a habit." - Aristotle

C onsistency is a significant ingredient of excellence. Being consistent means staying fully engaged without getting distracted, and it's also the ability to remain dedicated to a goal, an activity, or a task. Consistency has to do with being responsible for your actions, decisions, choices and also being reliable. When you're consistent, it means that until the moment your objectives are achieved, you'll keep following through with what you plan. And this is usually a sign that you're a person of your words. Over the long-term, you must stay true to a sustained practice — there's a level of commitment you must give in to be consistent.

You can think of consistency as the act of doing some little things every day; these little things get to form your routine, and this routine helps you build the habits that will propel you towards achieving your goal. Consistency is the key to high levels of achievement; it is one of the major things that separates successful people from failed people, and it's simply all about repetition. Because, in going through the same actions, you'll get to gain better insights to do things better, and as you keep going, you keep growing, discovering new grounds, and achieving more success.

Three Pillars of Consistency

1. Value: You stand a high chance of delivering the same value in your tasks if you stay consistent in your efforts and action. In fact, there will be an improvement in your weight.

2. Patience: If success has always been your number one goal in life, you need to be patient and focused. Even if success is not your number one priority, but you have the eagerness to be successful, you'll still need to be patient as you keep striving day by day. And you'll be able to manage your output with consistent efforts, regardless of the amount of work involved.

3. Belief: Our belief shapes our lives. Every time you take up a task, you'll be motivated to deliver results by consistency in your thoughts.

Consistency is Key to Success

The importance of consistency cannot be underrated. While many think that consistency is just a word with no big deal, others who value its weighty significance understand that it's a virtue worth emulating. Consistency is a common factor across leaders in all fields, and one thing that will help you succeed in this life is to be consistent in your routine. When you ask successful athletes across many sports how they could emerge victoriously, one thing they'll tell you is how consistent they can be with their training and their dedication to keep moving. Consistency helps to achieve success, and without mincing words, it's a cogent virtue that will help you climb the ladder of success.

When we were younger, you would remember vividly that our teachers let us know how important it is to be consistent in what we do and what we're known for. But, it often seems that most of us only value the importance of consistency when we enter the adult world because we don't take our childhood thoughts too seriously, and it's often because we are busying enjoying life and moments. Honestly, we cannot blame ourselves or hold on to the guilt of the past, but as we advance in life, we must find our energy and channel our inner drive to move consistently. If you do not have consistent efforts as backup, you realize that the motivation of inspiration you're relying on to help you do what you should do may not last long.

Your excitement may fizzle out, and the short-term failures you got from the project you're working on may demoralize you. But, one thing about consistency is that it can serve as a source of motivation for you to push deadlines while working, it can fuel your passion, it will help you have a better understanding of what works and what does not, and you'll be encouraged to have the will to learn from your mistakes. If you're consistent in your efforts, losing the passion for pursuing a project because of few setbacks is something you may never experience because your focus will often be on how to turn things around for the better since you're not planning to quit halfway.

One story that explains how tangible and valuable consistency is; is the fable of the tortoise and the hare. Everyone knows tortoise has a languid pace and the hare, of course, a foster animal. So, there was a race challenge between the two animals, and many of the audience, in their minds, already knew who the winner would be. As expected, the hare was leading in the race because he was fast and competent. However, he became too overconfident that he took a nap, believing that he could always dash off past the tortoise whenever he was awake.

At first, Tortoise exercised a leap of faith in his abilities and showed belief (a lesson that everyone should learn) because, typically, he should have rejected the duel. After all, it was never a competition. Second, remember that the hare was already leading him with a considerable margin, but did he give up? No, he didn't! He stayed in his lane, moving, persevering, taking a step at a time, pushing, striving, advancing. And eventually, he got to reach the finish line while the other party was still catching some sleep. He stayed consistent in his efforts and was firmly determined to get to the finish line. This story tells us that no goal is impossible to achieve if you're consistent. Look at the famous, successful billionaires you see today. Most of them are now renowned and incredibly established because they didn't give up on the dream they had. They kept moving and pushing and stayed consistent.

Consistency is crucial, and here are some reasons:

1. It leads to self-discipline. Self-discipline is essential to succeed, and you can learn to be disciplined by working consistently to achieve your goal as you stay committed to it. To succeed, you must develop self-discipline. It's very vital, and several leadership gurus have always been mentioning how significant it is.

2. It teaches self-control. There is a high possibility of losing focus on your goal if you cannot manage your emotions in tough times. Before you make it to the top, you'll encounter several challenges and difficult situations because the road to success isn't easy nor smooth. However, you can channel your energy to keep going and be motivated to control your emotions when you're committed to your goal, especially in tough times. Consistency teaches your commitment.

3. It helps to build momentum. Consistency motivates you to work tirelessly, and it also helps you build passion concurrently. Since you're being committed to a cause as a consistent fellow, you have a high tendency to feel good about what you're working on, and this will always help you overcome an array of challenges that you'll meet. Consistency breeds momentum that will empower you in the sight of obstacles.

4. It improves your personality. Your abilities improve when you practice consistency and add virtues such as confidence, hard work, and discipline, reflecting your nature. To climb the ladder of success quickly, you shouldn't forget that you need consistency.

5. It creates a sense of accountability. Celebrate your wins and all your efforts that have amounted to something nice because of your consistency. Do well to look back and enjoy the success when your character pays off, and you can always make amends by evaluating your actions and taking a step back if the results are not as good as you'd expected.

6. Sense of measurement. Consistently trying something is a great way to know if something works for you or it doesn't.

7. Be noticed. You're bound to achieve results if your efforts are consistent, and you're working hard. It's just as the famous saying goes, "Hard work never goes unnoticed," and this is pretty much true. You can stand out for outstanding achievements and be bound to get noticed as you carve your path to success with the milestones you create with consistency.

8. It builds trust. An excellent way for you to gain the confidence of your clients or customers is by staying consistent. For instance, let's say you're into a particular business and your customers appreciate your service, but there was a glitch at a point in time. Now, there are usually two options you can choose from; you may choose to avoid and deny the glitch and shy away from it or step up to make amends. Business owners who believe in consistency and value its significance will always choose the latter option; they'll rise to fix the loophole. With this, they understand that they'll win more trust from the people patronizing them, and their customers will even appreciate them more.

9. It teaches you to overcome challenges. Life is a classroom. We learn every day from different situations and different people, regardless of age differences. Consistent people have the drive and momentum to keep pressing after a few challenges, but inconsistent fellows will permanently retire from the race before it ends. To continue with consistent efforts, you must be self-disciplined and continue trials, even though challenges are the idea behind the concept of consistency.

10. Passion and motivation. One of the beautiful things about consistency is that it will constantly fuel you to explore great ideas and opportunities. You'll always feel motivated to push your limits if you're continually working towards achieving a cause or a goal.

The 3cs of Consistency; What Consistency Involves.

Curiosity, communication, and confidence are the 3cs of consistency, and we all have them embedded in us. However, a subset of characteristics accompanies these three significant traits, and these subsets help us a lot in our business operations.

Here are the subsets of the 3cs:

- **Positivity**: For you to achieve your vision, it's pertinent that you have a positive mindset. Positivity will make you move forward consistently, and it's the only way you can keep seeing the good in the bad.

- **Persistence**: Your goals and objectives cannot be achieved if you're not persistent. Persistence and consistency are pretty much synonyms, but the significant difference is that the word "persistence" carries a sense of strength and vigor to push through a phase or keep pushing through until it achieves success.

- **Challenges**: To succeed, there will be hurdles you'll need to jump over, and you'll face some challenges from outsiders or competitors.

- **Risk-taking**: Before you can grow as a human or even grow your business, you must take reasonable and positive risks.

- **Mistakes**: To progress in life and learn what not to do, you need to make mistakes. Successful people aren't scared of making mistakes because they believe it's a launching pad for success.

- **Learning**: You need to be curious about the world around you to keep learning, and you must keep on learning because we're all lifelong learners in this world.

- **Desire**: For you to aim higher and achieve your vision, you need to desire it.

- **Hope**: Until you desire, you may never know what hope is. Desire brings hope, and hope gives you the strength to persist on the journey.

- **Courage**: To be incited to work towards achieving your vision, you need to be courageous.

- **Love**: It's imperative that you love yourself and you love how unique you are. On days when you're down, self-love will be there to cheer you on, and the love you give to others and receive will also play a significant role.

- **Trust**: You need to believe that you can do it. You should trust your gut. Trust your knowledge. Trust your ability. Believe and trust yourself.

- **Freedom**: There's this sense of freedom you'll get when you've achieved what you want to or when you're getting excellent results.

- **Happy**: You'll be able to become prosperous, help others, and be able to support others when you find yourself-worth, self-confidence. Care for yourself and love yourself. And above all, happiness is usually a byproduct of freedom.

- **Loyalty**: cooperation, trust, willingness, and hard work are all ingrained in commitment, and with consistency comes belief.

Why is Consistency Difficult?

Most people struggle to stay consistent, even when they trivialize it as something straightforward. Such people find it gruesome to practice consistency because they find it herculean to stick with something because of their lack of discipline and absence of commitment and sense of focus. More so, the plenty of distractions also make some people struggle to stay consistent. People who see no reason to continue with some actions over the long haul because they cannot get immediate results from their efforts only live for the short-term and such people often find it hard to stay consistent over the long term.

Consistency is about improving as time goes on and making incremental progress. And, it isn't about getting quick results. In this world we live in today, where everything is fast-paced, most people struggle to be consistent in what they do because they cannot accept that some things take time but would instead focus on looking for instant gratification. And, all these explain why it's been difficult for some people to practice consistency.

Tips to Stay Consistent

If we'll be honest and factual, one thing most people struggle with is consistency. And, this lack of consistency kills dreams, potentials, great ideas, and unique initiatives. You can transform your life beyond your imagination if only you can brace yourself up to follow some of your life's callings and be consistent. Here are some tips that can help you be status consistent;

1. If you really want to do it, commit yourself fully to it. You need to ask yourself if you really want to do something before you commit yourself to it. How important is that thing to you? One problem most people make is using the face value of items to determine their level of commitment and staying committed to items in the heat of the moment. And this is often because they're not conscious of what it takes to remain committed to getting the desired result and don't take time to think things through. Before you commit yourself to any important thing; ask yourself these questions;

- What is my honest WHY behind wanting this?
- Am I doing this just in the heat of the moment?
- Do I really want to do this?

- Am I willing to give it all it takes? What if I'll have to sacrifice a few things along the line? Can I do that?
- Am I willing to take time out for this?
- Am I ready and eager to develop all the skills and go through the learning curve?
- If there are challenges ahead, am I willing to face them?

2. Practice the act of focusing on one thing at a time. One reason most people fail at consistency is because they bite more than chew. They're the same people that want to do this and do another and be seen almost everywhere, and because their energy is getting directed towards different areas, they get worn out easily and find it challenging to be consistent. In fact, sticking to developing one habit is a good habit you should create. You can focus on skill and develop your mastery level if it's a skill you're working on, and if it's a business, focus on one idea at first and keep working on it. Chasing other ideas simultaneously will affect your consistency in the main idea you're working on currently.

3. Make it sustainable and straightforward; don't complicate. There's nothing beautiful about complications. It's usually too disorienting. Quit the habit of making things more complex than they should. Quit the habit of getting into tiny details and too much fuss when you're planning to start something. Understand that simplicity is the key to sustainability. Keep it simple, and it is easy to sustain. This is very important because after the initial hype fades off, it will be difficult for you to last long if you're fretting over tiny details, trying to make everything perfect, and getting into too much detail in the beginning. Carrying on in the rough patches will be pretty much harder if you've complicated things and make them look too tricky because, typically, along the way, there will always be that difficulty you'll experience. Get in the habit of getting things going, and as you progress, you can level things and keep adding the details.

4. Choose and prioritize efficiency. The idea of you choosing efficiency is that you don't work up yourself too much over trying to be creative. Sure, creativity is good and highly recommended, but you understand it can affect your sustainability level in the long run, and the efficiency and flow of things can be affected by unnecessary creativity. Creativity has its own place, and it's undoubtedly a must in the right place but, if you know you don't want to waste your mental energy on little things, choose flow and efficiency in routine tasks. Particularly when you're just starting, efficiency should be your primary concern. Wasting your creative efforts on petty things isn't ideal at all. As you progress, you'll start doing more things that matter, and this is when you can now joyfully use your reserved mental energy and creativity. The simple idea is to stick to the basics and be consistent, and as you progress, you can now start implementing creative ideas.

5. Avoid "Paralysis by Analysis." Too much of everything is terrible, and this also extends to analysis. Let me tell you, you'll get fed up and eventually give up when you overthink things, particularly when you're yet to be getting any results and you're just getting started. The internet doesn't even make things easier for anyone these days; with the plenty of information out there, it's easy for one to drown in confusion while perusing all the found details and analysis. Understand that things take time, and if you're not getting results right away, don't fret. Focus all your energy on delivering as you seek a solid strategy with enough information. In the long run, you'll be able to sky-rocket your progress, and you'll be able to focus on delivering your best and have more peace of mind during the process when you stop analyzing too much. Don't give in two doubts and negative thoughts, especially all those thoughts that drop in one's mind with "what if..."

6. Set realistic goals and expectations. Anthony Robbins once said that many people underestimate what they can do in a decade and overestimate what they can do in a year. And, this is actually very true because it's easy for you to talk to someone who'll be gladly overestimating what they can get done in less than a year. People expect results too early, especially when they've seen or heard about the overnight success stories of other people. However, what they are oblivious to is that blowing up overnight isn't the norm. It's an exceptional case. Things take time to develop. Encourage the habit of setting realistic goals and expectations even as you aim the highest.

7. Pace yourself to avoid burnout. You need to be conscious of avoiding burnout because there's the propensity to work too hard to the point of burnout during the initial hype of things. Do well to refresh your mind and spirits by switching things up a little. Along the way, relax, enjoy, and take some time to breathe. Don't forget to pace yourself while you're working hard. You may even oblige to going to a mini vacation on the weekend because making yourself available to take an opportunity to fully unwind, relax or take a complete break is part of pacing yourself. You'll notice that you'll feel ready, refreshed, rejuvenated, and more inspired once you get back to your routine.

8. Value progress over perfection. Is there even anything like perfection? Well, you tell me if the model is more like an illusion, and even if you want to attain perfection, you should know that it will take years, a very long time. There's a likelihood that your inner critic and perfectionist will pinpoint all your errors and flaws to you when you enthusiastically start on something. However, while that is pretty much likely to happen, you must learn to tell your inner critic to sit down and stop fretting. Sometimes we'll mess things up. This is not a big deal, and it's okay to make mistakes, and again, items don't always have to go smoothly as we'd expected. Understand that you cannot always give your best all the time, and an unproductive and inefficient mindset you shouldn't have is a mindset of "all or nothing."

9. To be consistent, you must learn to say no. Most times, we're often occupied by unnecessary things, which is one reason it's often hard for us to be consistent. A vital part of being consistent is learning to say NO. Say no to anything that might get in the way as you stay focus on your priority list and remain committed to whatever it is you want to commit to. Avoid making promises you can't keep and know that it's easy for you to be dragged away from your priority tasks by distractions when you refuse to prioritize.

10. Accept your imperfections and forgive yourself. Your perception about consistency will have to be reshaped if you think that the ability to never falter ever again is what being consistent means. As a human, there's always that time that you will lapse. Nothing is 100% perfect, and we all have our difficulties. You might give up and feel disappointed in yourself when you go too hard on yourself. It's good to be ambitious, but letting it reach a stage that profoundly affects you can be counter-productive. If you get off track, how fast you come back to your commitment matters, and how perfectly you follow through determines your consistency. It's totally natural for life to influence how you commit, and it's understandable. However, what's important is that you get back to it, forgive yourself, accept it, and don't beat yourself up.

11. Create a system and automate your work. Rather than getting worked up over the tiny details every time you do something or think about the order of things, make everything stick by setting a specific system, and this can be pretty helpful for you whenever you're hoping to achieve consistency in your professional or your personal life. In fact, we can put an unnecessary hassle that could overwhelm you off when you put a system in place because you won't have to worry about everyday stuff or waste your mental energy thinking. Technology has even made things easier. Explore technology to your advantage and, through apps and online services, automate as many items as you can. You'll be able to free up a lot of time, be saved from being overwhelmed, and get your life simplified with automation. Even if you're not a tech-savvy person, you can always brace yourself up to get used to any automation app or service.

Habits to Practice and Build Consistency

1. Show up no matter what. You won't get what you want if you quit halfway through, but you'll be confirming that you really want something by showing up at every chance you get. Consistency will gather your success for you, whether you're on the quest for your dream job and you're going to repeat interviews, or you're writing that book for the next 10 years.

2. Set reminders. Always be conscious about the significance of being consistent and don't cannot remind yourself about your goals.

3. Practice appreciation. Always appreciate your efforts. You're likely to repeat a behavior if you feel excellent, and acknowledging it makes one feel good. For the hard work invested, appreciate yourself for that, regardless of what the result says.

4. Take feedback. Don't be arrogant about taking feedback. Take it and learn from it.

5. Use motivational tools/support. You can enjoy continuity to work towards your goal when you explore external instruments to your advantage. You may be low on motivation, and the support you get and your motivation tools can always boost your energy.

6. Keep a schedule. Remind yourself of pending tasks and visit your schedule at regular intervals. Know that whenever you plan to achieve your goal, you need to maintain a program, and mind you, the goals must be realistic.

7. **Eliminate negative thoughts**. Stop giving in to negative vibes and thoughts. Convince your mind to be consistent by channeling your positive thoughts towards it

Reflection:

> ➤ Look at your goals again

> ➤ What do you need to do to achieve them? What repetitive actions or activities are required?

> ➤ What specific habits or rituals can you develop to support these actions?

> ➤ When will I partake in these activities? How? When exactly? How often?

> ➤ What repetitive activities must I avoid doing?

Chapter 7: Secret 4– There's Always a Solution

A person who sees a problem is a human being; a person who finds a solution is a visionary, and the person who goes out and does something about it is an entrepreneur.–Naveen Jain

In this life that we're in, we're bound to face unique problems at different junctures of our lives, especially whenever we're journeying to achieve success. Issues play a significant role in who we become, and they're an integral part of our lives, whether we accept them. There will be unique problems we'll face from time to time in our lives, but in dealing with these problems, there are two significant kinds of mindsets that play out. The first one is the mindset of expecting the pain to go away. This kind of mindset makes you ignore the problem, constantly complain about why the issue came up, and shifts all your focus to the problem.

Despite ignoring the problem, the problem never goes, and it could keep compounding, building more force, and growing stronger until you'll eventually have no choice than just to deal with it. This kind of mindset is called a problem-oriented mindset. However, when you have a problem or problems, and you're already thinking of solving them by breaking them into smaller parts and connecting the dots, refusing to be overwhelmed by the size, not lamenting on the situation, but thinking about the potential solutions to the problems, this is a solution-based or solution-oriented mindset. You'll feel motivated and empowered to solve an array of situations when you have a solution-oriented mindset.

If you want to be more capable of changing the situations in your life and feel happier, practice and inculcate solution-oriented thinking. Focusing on solutions makes you feel empowered, but you'll feel powerless when you focus too much on a problem. Find answers by activating your critical thinking skills instead of lamenting over the situation whenever you have issues. There's usually a solution to every problem, and there can even be over one solution. But it could be unfortunate that many prefer to lament over their issues instead of taking charge.

Here are a few scenarios that illustrate the approach of a solution-oriented mindset and a problem-based mindset;

- Problem-oriented: There is no way I can afford this.
- Solution-oriented: Is there a way I can afford this?
- Problem-oriented: I'm stuck. I am clueless about what to do.
- Solution-oriented: I need to sit and relax and then think about what to do to move forward.
- Problem-oriented: Why did they get that? That is not fair at all.
- Solution-oriented: Is there a way I can make myself available for this opportunity? Maybe they'll be willing to give me some hints. Let me try to ask.
- Problem-oriented: I wish I could go to college and become an educated professional.
- Solution-oriented: Is there anything I can do to raise money or get a scholarship so I can make my dream come true?

People who are problem-oriented thinkers have a few traits in common, and here are some of them;

- Quick to give up
- Easily frustrated
- Often place blame on others
- Feeling hopeless
- Negative

Likewise, solution-oriented thinkers also have a few traits in common, and here are some of them:

- Willing to hold on until we solve a problem
- See problems as challenges that can be overcome
- Take responsibility
- Optimistic and feeling hopeful
- Positive

We can solve the most challenging problems with creative solutions when our mind is engaged in its total capacity. Our reason is a powerful tool, and excellent solutions can flow more freely when you find that new place of calm because all the change you may need may just be changing the way you think about a situation.

Solution-based Thinking is Critical to Success

I often find it is interesting when people don't want to develop a solution or come up with a solution, but prefer to complain about a problem constantly or keep presenting problems. It's easy for anyone to point out a problem; anyone can highlight a problem, but what's the value that lies in discovering problems without thinking of ways to solve them? People who have a problem-oriented mindset tend to not allow for robust solutions. They can hinder the promotion of team spirit and even foster animosity within a team.

There's often no value offered by problem discoverers because frequently, all the accolades go to the solution providers, and this is a clear affirmation that having solution-based thinking is vital to achieving success. Of course, it's good to raise issues or problems, but getting engaged in solving issues by offering the willingness to execute proposed ideas and even coming to the table with solutions; if you're working with a team. Questions like "what part do you play in the problem," "how can you help to resolve the issue," "how can you get involved," and "what are your thoughts on the issue" are some questions you can ask your workers or colleagues if there's a concern elevated, to foster a solution-based mindset.

People with a solution-oriented mindset often provide a better way of doing things. They help identify the source of a question, and they don't just solve problems, and these help them achieve success quickly. Solution-oriented people often get things done right. They always answer the 'why' question, use critical thinking, and always find a way. Since problems are an inevitable part of life, companies, organizations, and industries are often looking for solution providers, and if, as a person, you're still trapped in a problem-based mindset, it will be pretty tricky for you to be exceptional.

Here are a few more reasons you must have solution-based thinking;

- **It reduces stress**. Your physical and mental health can benefit when you are optimistic because having a solution-based mindset means that you're optimistic; you see the good in the bad. Your stress level is associated with your state of mind, and you can enjoy reduced stress and better health when you develop a positive mindset.

- **It helps you make better financial decisions**. As an optimist, you'll often be thinking about ways to profit, but you'll always be working yourself up on trying to avert disaster, living in a defensive mode, and focusing on adverse outcomes if you're a pessimist with a problem-based mindset. Though it's good to analyze, you're less likely to make intelligent financial decisions if you have a problem-based attitude.

- **The entrepreneurial mindset**. You'll never start a business in the first place if what can go wrong is all you think about. To be an entrepreneur, you must be an optimist because businesses naturally thrive on optimism.

- **More sales**. As a business owner, there will be several problems from customers you'll have to deal with, but you'll always be able to make more sales when you develop and foster a solution-based mindset.

Successful Businesses Solve Problems

Every business primarily exists to solve problems. As the world evolves every day with several new ideas and innovations, it's pretty simple: people are constantly looking for smarter, faster, and better ways to get things done. And likewise, consumers will always be on the lookout for solutions, as long as they have problems. As an entrepreneur, you should be able to work on improving your existing products, and you should as well have it registered in your mind that your capacity to keep solving your customers' problems consistently and even more innovatively is what will keep you at the top of the business success ladder

As a business owner, here are a few things you should note as you intend to cultivate a solution-based mindset;

1. Shift your attention from having an excellent product to building a must-have product. For you to thrive excellently in this world, you must do something different and better. Although it could be pretty challenging to fully satisfy the needs of consumers because of the usual demand for quicker and faster results, you should know that only a few products are getting noticed in this era of multitasking that we're in, and more so, attention spans are getting shorter. Customers are usually faced with several options every blessed day, and because they will always expect and demand more, you must work on building must-have products and not just having another excellent product. Do you ever wonder why apps and software programs keep having updated versions? It's simply because of the significance of serving consumers better, knowing that their desires will be more and their expectations will keep increasing, even if they enjoy using the app or software a lot.

2. Solve real painful problems. Know that wants rarely make the cut. You need to solve the needs of your customers if you're going to grab their attention. Sit down to think and reflect on what you can make better or brighter. Think of it, Uber is working on improving car service, Netflix solved on-demand streaming media, online buying and selling have been simplified by Amazon, Google even made search better. Now, how are you planning to make your products or services better?

3. Your business should be your passion. Passion is a vital ingredient for success, and you must start a dynamic business. To make it as an entrepreneur, you need to persevere, be committed, and be inspired. And, it's usually easy to give your all to something that you're passionate about. You must be, in fact, obsessed with solving a significant problem, something you hold dearly.

4. Just as you're passionate, you must also can execute. To increase your chances of success, you need to focus on solving a real problem people actually have. Don't just start another business just because you're passionate about it. Make plans. Ensure you have a real market for your idea, validate your vision, and do your homework thoroughly.

Starting a business that may not survive is something you wouldn't want to do, and this explains how pertinent it is to put execution into cognizance.

Get Creative and Think Outside the Box

Creative problem solving, also shortly known as CPS, helps people overcome obstacles and reach their goals. Creative problem solving helps people come up with innovative solutions and encourages people to find fresh perspectives. When conventional thinking has failed, CPS helps identify opportunities, and it's a way of solving problems. Creative problem solving is all about thinking outside the box, thinking beyond the superficial, and connecting yourself to a more profound sense and understanding.

Whether you're a business owner or a leader, you must learn to think outside of the box and get creative — this is crucial. You need to find innovative solutions that work and encourage creative thinking if you want your organization to excel and improve your interpersonal skills, communications, services, and products. It's a regular part of working life to deal with obstacles and challenges, and even though it may not always be easy to overcome them, we must get creative at solving problems.

Core Principles of Creative Problem Solving

There are four core principles of creative problem solving, and they are;

1. **Balance divergent and convergent thinking**. Most times, we develop new ideas or solutions by using both divergent and convergent thinking. When you're analyzing your options, and you're going for the one that seems more promising, that's convergent thinking. However, when you're brainstorming; generating lots of potential solutions and possibilities. That's divergent thinking. You can stifle idea generation and arrive at unbalanced or biased decisions when you use both divergent and convergent thinking simultaneously. For CPS, you need to know when to practice either of the two, and you must also learn to identify and balance the two.

2. **Ask problems as questions**. It's easier to come up with solutions when you reword problems and challenges as questions. You'll be able to generate adequate rich information when you ask these types of questions. However, there's a tendency to develop limited responses to problem statements and elicit short answers, like disagreements or confirmations, when you ask closed questions.

3. **Defer or suspend judgment**. Hold on. Don't judge yet. During the convergence stage, you'll find an apt time to consider ideas. There's a high tendency of you

shutting down idea generation when you judge solutions early.

4. **Focus on "Yes, and," rather than "No, but."** In generating information and ideas, you must be very conscious of your expressions because language matters. And, there's a high chance of you negating or even ending the conversation when you use the word "yes but" or "no but..

Common Traits of Good Problem Solvers

1. They know what the problem is. Before others do, they can spot specific or hindrances in many situations.

2. They know when to apply complex or straightforward solutions. They're pretty conscious of finding an easier route to the solution by using shortcuts or attacking the issue with systematic and complex solutions.

3. They view problems as opportunities to grow. They improve on their existing expertise by seeing problems as situations that open windows of learning opportunities.

4. They are creative. They're not ordinary, casual thinkers. They think differently and delve beyond what is most apparent.

5. They don't feel that they are always right. Good problem solvers will never brag. Proving someone else wrong or proving themselves right isn't usually their goal because their attention is on what's best for the present circumstance.

6. They have well-developed social skills. They use this as an opportunity to harness their channels for solutions. Both in-person and online, they connect well with people.

7. They would instead prevent then intervene. Often entirely centered on quality and due diligence, they're very apt in preventing problems from developing in the first place because they understand how important prevention is better than cure.

8. They explore all options. They often have a new angle towards handling an issue, and they're always ready with a backup plan as trouble-shooters. Most times, they barely rely solely on a single solution.

9. They have reasonable expectations in specific situations. They use realistic expectations to approach each problem and understand the importance of patience, considering that a problem might be caused by several issues.

10. They don't create more problems for other people. They're very conscious about the solution they provide so that these solutions wouldn't turn out as an inconvenience or cause harm to others.

Steps of Creative Problem Solving

1. Clarify and identify the problem. What you solidly think is the problem or goal may not be the real problem, and therefore identifying your actual issue or destination is a significant step of creative problem-solving.

- **Five whys: A powerful problem-definition technique**. For you to clarify the real issues behind the problem, you need to ask yourself a series of questions, and if you don't want to ask yourself, you may request a family member or a friend to ask you questions for this will help you understand the underlying issues better and clarify the problem. In using the Five whys, "why do I wish to achieve this goal?" or "why is this a problem?" is the first question you'll have to ask. After you've answered that, you'll explore the other four reasons by asking "why else?" which helps to give you five whys in total. For example, let's say you have anger issues. And, you asked yourself the first why; "why is this a problem?" and your response is "because I can't control my emotions." Once you've answered that, you'll ask yourself, "Why else?" four times, and your responses may be "because I don't feel happy about how my life is going," "because I'm underpaid and I'm often frustrated," "because I find it difficult to express myself without getting angry," and "because my wife offended me a long time ago and I'm yet to forgive her." Pressing more beyond your first why will help you see the origin of that problem beyond what you see on the surface.

- **More questions you can ask to help to get the problem defined clearly**. Questions like: "Are my friends or any of my family members dealing with this same problem? "If they are, how are they managing it?", "When I solve this problem, where do I see myself in the next few months or years?" What's hindering me from solving this problem?" "What do I really wish to accomplish?". You should have a clear idea of what your problem is once you've answered all these questions.

- **Set criteria for judging potential solutions**. In evaluating or considering the ideas, this is where you have to decide on the criteria you'll use. Can a timeframe or budget limitations affect your plans to go ahead with an idea? When you implement these ideas, what do you wish to avoid? What do you plan to achieve with the ideas?

2. Research the problem. Your favorite search engine is usually the best place to start your research these days. And, you may need to do just very little or a great deal of research, depending on the problem. For you to have a better understanding of it, you must research the problem. Family, colleagues, and friends can provide thoughts on many issues. For in-depth information, you can visit the libraries. Old-fashioned sources of opinion and sources aren't bad ideas too.

3. Formulate one or more creative challenges. Focusing on a single issue, creative challenges should be concise and straightforward. A simple question framed to foster ideas or suggestions is a creative challenge.

4. Generate ideas. Write everything down, no exceptions. Don't make yourself less creative by squelching your own ideas. Don't be your own worst critics; write it down, even if your idea doesn't solve the challenge or you feel it's stupid or ridiculous. You must write every statement that comes to mind. And, you can use specialized software for idea generation, enter them onto a computer document like OpenOffice or MS Word, write them down on a mind map, or simply write them down linearly. Do well to write your ideas on a document, regardless of your approach to idea generation. You can generate ideas while walking, sitting down in a coffee shop on a crowded street corner, chilling in a nice place in a beautiful park, or taking a trip somewhere for new inspiration. Know that your desk isn't necessarily where your brainstorming must occur.

5. Combine and evaluate ideas. You can form big ideas by combining related ideas. Go through the ideas. It might take you a day or more, or maybe just an hour. Just take a break after you're done writing all of your ideas so you can have time to prep for evaluation. Don't feel reluctant about including your favorite ideas in the initial list of ideas, and take note you could end up choosing the less creative ideas if the "best" ideas or your favorite ideas are the only ones you focus on — this is very important. To solve your challenge, you can consistently implement several ideas so, you don't need to limit yourself to one winning idea.

6. Draw up an action plan. It can be pretty intimidating to implement ideas that involve a lot of work, but you need to develop an action plan with the simple steps you must take to implement your thoughts. In a world where some people are scared by risk and change, others find these two lovable. You may need to take the chance of changing follow through with creative ideas. You must motivate yourself to take the next step because you've already got some great ideas. And, also take note your ideas will be easier to cope with and implement when you break down their implementation process into more straightforward tasks.

7. Do it! Go for it; go implement your idea, take your action plan. This is the most straightforward step. Have it registered in your mind that you can always rewrite your action plan if you find it necessary?

Tips to Improve Your Problem-Solving Skills

Develop a step-by-step approach. Separate the symptoms from the cause and avoid focusing on the wrong problem because there could be multiple issues within one situation. Start with identifying the problem and form a strategy. The problem-solving cycle is another name this approach is called.

Organize your information. You'll be increasing your chances of achieving a positive outcome when you collect as much information as possible.

Evaluate the result. Measure your solution against your goals and if you realize it wasn't successful, do well to use a distinct approach next time.

Ask solution-oriented questions. Ask the right questions. An essential part of our daily lives is asking questions, but make sure the questions propel you to find solutions.

Change your mindset. You'll be less stressed about finding a solution if you change your perspective to view challenges as an opportunity for growth. Avoid dwelling on negative first impressions and focus on improvements.

Work with your hands. Do you know that manipulating a Rubik's cube, playing Sudoku, or chess can help in improving your problem-solving skills as an adult? Well, now you know.

Ask for help. Seek support and encouragement from family and friends. You can even get fresh ideas when you work with others. Ask others for help. Put your ego aside.

Reflect and celebrate. Sometimes an issue will stress you. At that moment, just try to get engaged in something you enjoy so you can loosen up. You can call a friend, read a book, meditate, or read. And when you're calm, you can now return to the situation with a positive attitude.

Habits to Practice

1. Explore a question. From making a significant financial decision and choosing a clothing color to everything from easy and complex tasks, develop solid questioning habits. Critical thinkers ask lots of questions.

2. Manage an ordered list. You'll be able to accomplish more because everything just feels better when we have a sense of order. You can make a complicated day more streamlined when you organize tasks and set their level of priority.

3. Engage in a conversation. Conversation helps you challenge viewpoints and bold new ideas, and it can involve solid action planning, impactful learning, and deep listening in the end.

4. Pinpoint a weakness and plan to improve it. Start taking small steps to make an improvement happen as you think of an area of your life that needs improvement. Our weak points can continuously be improved upon, and we all have our strengths and weaknesses.

5. Set a goal. For setting goals for themselves, critical thinkers are prudent and patient. You'll strive to push yourself to be more than you are when you have plans. To lead a successful and fulfilling life, you must build the habit of setting goals.

6. Keep emotions out of it. Avoid magnifying your problems by getting tunnel-visioned. There's a solution for every situation. Remember this, always.

7. Identify causes, the root cause, especially. Consider other views and opinions. If you knew how to solve it, it wouldn't be considered a 'problem.' Play the devil's advocate. Look at the problem from diverse angles. Think of how and why it happened.

8. Gather many facts. You'll be capable of resolution when you're informed. Gather facts based on evidence.

9. Brainstorm solutions. Gather solid facts and define the problem clearly before you brainstorm.

10. Learn something new. Visit a blog, listen to a podcast, or watch an online tutorial. Read a book or magazine that interests you, a breaking news story, or learn something in a random conversation. There are several ways to learn, and one of the most essential critical thinking habits you can develop is keeping your mind fresh and young by learning. No matter where we are in life, there's always something new to discover, and we never stop learning throughout our lives.

Reflection:

➤ Think about the annoying problems you have in life or concerns that you keep hearing other people complaining about

➤ How can you help solve this problem for them?

➤ Will they pay you for this help? If not, how can you monetize it?

Chapter 8: Secret 5–No Man Is an Island

No one succeeds alone, and no one fails alone. Pay attention to the people around you.–Gary W. Keller

Your success in life depends on people, and you should start working on yourself if you're someone who's developed a penchant for living without associating or cooperating with other people. Without the help and support of other people, success is impossible. This is not a negative declaration or affirmation; it's the most straightforward, most accurate reality. People help people succeed. No one gets to the top without being helped. At a particular point in your life, it's the people you have in your life that will stand for you, and the relationships you've built with people can open several doors for you. Thus, you must live responsibly and give generously, and you see good things will come your way eventually.

When you're good to people, people will also be good to you. In fact, whenever you're down or stuck, and you need help, you'll see people around you trying to reciprocate the good deeds you've done to them because you've helped them to advance in their lives and encouraged them. If there are people around you, inspire them to succeed. Encourage them. Assist them. Being the one helping others is a surefire way to get people to help you. And, even if you have no means to help or assist people, remember that this doesn't stop you from being friendly and kind to people and building good relationships with people wherever you meet. Always be conscious that we're all social beings as humans, and we need each other to survive. The politicians depend on voters to vote for them, and the voters depend on politicians to make society a better place. The seller is looking for a buyer, and the buyer needs what the seller is selling. In fact, even the wealthiest persons in the world are often reliant on a team to thrive and accomplish their dreams.

Our capabilities and skills often get broadened by others, and no one can make it alone. Many of us admire celebrities when we see them or even hear about them, but if you notice, you'll realize that they're usually quick to thank their fans, their teams, and well-wishers for their support and encouragement. To achieve professional and personal goals in this life, you need the help of others. Needing the benefit of others doesn't make you a beggar; it's just the necessity of life for everybody, with no exceptions to any persons. Even the president of your country needs a Vice, and the Vice needs other people to work with, and it goes on like that. In fact, if you're observant, you would notice that politicians are professionals who value the significance of people a lot. These people have family members, coaches, mentors, and a team of individuals who are always rooting for them. Who are those rooting for you? What part have you played in people's lives?

The 10 People You Need to Be Successful

We all need to be motivated to continue pressing forward against all odds in this journey of life, and we need the company of people for this purpose. In this intricate journey of life, there will be times when we'll face moments of disappointment and experience failures, but despite the many twists turns we come across on this journey, the people we've built good relationships with can help to make things easier for us. Connections are necessary, even though they're difficult. And, know that everyone close to you serves a purpose, and while some special people might fill multiple roles for you, you should always be conscious of the fact that everyone around you is there to play a specific role in your life.

However, to reach your destination in life, there are distinct types of people that you need.

1. The Believer. This is the person who will be your positive force when negativity clouds your brain. This person knows your potential, he isn't afraid to speak up when you're wrong, and he's very realistic about your accomplishments. The

Believer knows where you started and where you are now, and this person can be your business partner, a colleague at work, best friend, spouse, or parent. The believer isn't someone that would come to fill your ears with pleasant things that will make you gush with excitement and blush, but the person is always there to remind you of your capabilities, especially when fear and self-doubt are clamping over your mind. The Believer is also your cheerleader. This person always tells you "sure you can do it," whether you're planning to invent something, go back to school, start a business, or do anything. This person encourages you to do whatever you want to do and thinks everything you do is incredible.

2. The Teacher. In this life, anyone can be your teacher. The person may be an elder person, a younger person, someone you know closely, or maybe someone you don't even know, but you constantly listen to the person's ideas and teachings. Always listen whenever The Teacher is speaking, because no matter how far you've come in life or how grown you are, you must keep learning. No one is above that. Your teacher can be someone in the cubicle next to you, a respected elder, someone from history, or an inspiring person whom you read their books to a lot. The Teacher can also be your mentor.

3. The Pusher. The Pusher can come in two different ways. Foremost, the person can be someone who pushes you to be better by example or someone who makes you better than they are. The Pusher encourages you to be a better person in your career, life, and relationship, and this is someone that inspires with fear and leads with an iron fist. The Pusher will teach you communication, kindness, patience, and a host of other virtues, and for some people, their pusher may be their parents, one of their relatives, or anybody at all that they hold in high esteem.

4. The Lover. We all need someone to love us. Even if the world turns on us, someone will be with us. Someone we can always share our feelings with without feeling timid; someone who gets us. This person will be your rock, someone you cherish so much, and someone you can have a conversation with within the middle of the night when you need to make a tough decision, and the person will always listen patiently. This person will help you strategize, re-prioritize, and re-evaluate, but you should also know that this person isn't someone that will just keep following you blindly on any path you choose. The Lover is someone who loves you and keeps your best interests at heart at all times. The Lover is your biggest supporter, but minds you, this person may not always be a romantic person, but it's often a romantic partner in most cases.

5. The Thinker. The Thinker balances out the dreamer in us. This person takes his time to gather facts, organize, and analyze them. He's a thinker, a watcher, and a listener. You can't measure this person's intelligence on an IQ scale, and funny enough, this person rarely feels the need to correct or give an opinion because he believes he's not a know-it-all. This person often seems to have all the answers, and he's someone you should include in all of your big decisions and listen to carefully.

6. The Achiever. This person is the mutual celebration when you succeed, the motivation when obstacles arise, and the photo on your vision board. This person stands up and finds his new strength instead of caving to the thought of I can't imagine when he experiences a setback in his career. One of the principal characters with The Achiever is his inability to accept failure and how he keeps pacing and advancing. The person could be a benchmark of success for you, your very dear friend, and someone who inspires you to dream bigger.

7. The Connector. This person can introduce you to the right people because he knows everyone and everyone knows him. When you have this kind of person in your life, you shouldn't be afraid to ask him for that introduction you need or desire because this person enjoys connecting with people in their network. This person can play a significant role in the expansion of connectivity and dynamism of your network. For your future success, you must have a super-connector in your network. This person is well-liked and probably has thousands of friends online who aren't random strangers but real friends.

8. The Idea Generator. This kind of person never runs out of ideas, and he's often eager to share them. Maybe you need solutions to problems or help with your business, writing, or art projects; he always has enough ideas to go around because he's an endless fountain of creative energy. This person has infectious enthusiasm, but while some of his ideas are great, some can be crazy.

9. The Optimist. You need this kind of person to see the positive angle from where you are standing, especially when you're feeling drained by obstacles and challenges. This person is usually there to let you know things will work out for good eventually, and the optimist can as well be a philosopher, a dreamer, or a realist. Above all, this person is more concerned about helping you focus on results rather than your limitations, and he makes you see a positive view so that you won't take the wrong turn.

10. The Anchor. The anchor can be your guiding force to achieving your dreams if you treat him right. This person understands when a great opportunity isn't great right now, knows your limits, and usually knows you better than you know yourself. This kind of person is often reliable, trusted, grounded, and realistic. The Anchor will tell you can't say yes to everything, but will not let you say no to a valuable opportunity that will immensely benefit your career. The anchor can be your personal assistant, your secretary, or someone who helps keep you organized.

Social Skills and its Significance

You'll be able to meet potential romantic partners in person, increase your friendship base, meet new people at parties, occasions, and functions, and make small talk with your coworkers if you have social skills. To have positive relationships with the people you care about and even with other people, you must set the proper foundation: social skills. The importance of social skills cannot be under-emphasized because they help you grow your relationship, help you have more in-depth relationships with others, and help you connect with other people on a better level. As a businessperson, it will be difficult for you to expand your network and meet new people if you find it herculean to interact appropriately with people, strangers in particular. And, if this is what you're experiencing, it's a clear sign that you have poor social skills.

To kick off a conversation with someone you find pretty, make friends, or meet new business partners, you must be able to approach people, and therefore social skills are beneficial — they allow you to start contact with people. People who have social skills enjoy being able to convey the right emotions. These kinds of people find it easy to connect with people emotionally, and they also exert the ability to express the feelings they want. Most people cannot convey the right emotions because of their poor social skills, making them uncomfortable while interacting with people. In fact, social skills furnish you with the capacity to know the needs and wants of people, give you the grace to sense how people feel, and even understand them more.

If you notice, many always love people with social skills. If you'd ask why, just think of how social skills help make people around you feel good, and since you can quickly meet and connect with people, there's no way the charm you ooze doesn't capture people. Businessmen and women who want to climb the ladder of success and move to the next level must find it needful to build social skills because they'll always be involved with people since their problem solvers.

To build healthy relationships, interact, and communicate, social skills are the tools we use.

Why It's Important to Have Good Social Skills

1. More Relationships. If you're not able to leverage relationships, it could be difficult for you to advance very far in life. You get relationships and even friendships, when you can identify with individuals. Take note that an extensive social network is proportional to satisfaction with life, and you'll enjoy a better outlook on life, make new friends, advance in your job, and even land a job (if you don't have a job) when you focus on relationships.

2. Great Communication Skills. You'll develop your communications skills when you can work in large groups and relate with people. Without excellent communications skills, having social skills is impossible, and also remember that every business that wants to grow and thrive must be able to communicate effectively.

3. More Efficiency. You enjoy more efficiency at what you do and who you are when you have social skills. With this, you can politely express yourself, you can make people like you, and you won't even have to dread social interactions.

4. A Better Career. As earlier noted, you need people to survive and be successful in life. Imagine you have poor social skills. How do you intend to communicate and relate with people? Now, do you see why social skills are very crucial? In fact, companies are often on the hunt for prospective employees who can influence people to get things done or possess a particular skill set. Even when you get employed at your job, given your lack of social skills, it could be pretty tricky for you to excel if you keep isolating yourself. There will always be colleagues, the media, employees, or even the target audience to talk to at several points, and without good social skills, you could flop badly.

5. Increased Quality of Life / Happiness. One thing that social skills help you achieve in this life is peace and happiness. How? Why? Good, I'll explain. Since you can express yourself, relate with people better, and even get loved by many because of social skills, you stand to enjoy happiness and a relaxed state of mind. Do you know you can get several personal and career-related doors opened up by getting along with people? Think about these things yourself.

Top Social Skill for Success

1. Effective communication. You can enjoy sharing your thoughts and ideas clearly with others when you have strong communication skills, and one of the core social skills is being able to communicate effectively with others. You can explain projects and goals in a way that's easy to understand and become a good leader if you're an effective communicator.

2. Conflict resolution. In any job, good conflict resolution skills are essential. You'll be able to find a workable solution and get to the source of the problem when you have conflict resolution skills. Disagreements and dissatisfaction are bound to occur anytime and to resolve conflicts. This skill is crucial, especially if your career is in HR.

3. Active listening. Because of the attention and respect active listeners offer others, they're used to be well-regarded and well-loved by people around them and their colleagues. Being able to listen attentively to who's communicating with you is active listening.

4. Empathy. You can build stronger, more respectful, and open relationships if you work on strengthening your empathy and rapport with others. Carefully considering how others will feel is the conscious effort it takes to be more empathetic, and people are more likely to confide in you if you have empathy.

Empathy has to do with your capacity to comprehend and identify with the feelings of someone.

5. Relationship management. Your professional relationships will flourish if you have this social skill. Your ability to build critical connections and maintain healthy relationships is what relationship management is about.

6. Respect. You can show respect by allowing people to speak without getting them interrupted in a team or group setting. Being conscious of when and how to start communication and respond is a crucial aspect of respect. Giving a rational response to questions you've been asked, asking straightforward questions, staying on topic, and using your time with someone else wisely are also ways to communicate respectfully.

Other social skills you should also have to include;

- **Optimism** — People are naturally drawn towards positive people because positivity works like a magnet.
- **Compassion** — Learn to have a deep desire to help people out and naturally feel for others.
- **Politeness** — Use words like "excuse me," "sorry," "thank you," and "please" often. Always avoid negative emotions or words and think twice about your words before you say them.

- **Emotional Intelligence** — Learn how to react better emotionally to people's emotions or situations.

- **Discipline** — Step out of your comfort zone, push yourself hard, change your routine, and don't wait for something to "feel right..

- **Diligence** — Know that nothing comes easy and there are no shortcuts in life.

- **Patience** — Practice patience by using meditative techniques instead of playing the blame game.

- **Affability** — Work on how well you get along with people. Respond appropriately, listen attentively, ask polite and relevant questions, and give a compliment.

- **Forgiveness** — Don't bear grudges and try to take things to heart, even though it's tricky to make peace with the pain.

- **Resilience** — Failure is not a dead end. It's only valuable feedback. No matter how testing an environment is, strive to survive and thrive.

- **Responsibility** — Own your actions.

- **Leadership** — Embrace change, align life's boundaries and values, and harness your interest, skills, and passion. Above all, "discover what's uniquely you..

- **Asking For Help** — solicit a helping hand.

- **Honesty** — Stay trustworthy.

Habits to Practice

Listen to people. You have a splendid chance of standing out from the crowd if you ask questions and listen, especially in a place where everyone is struggling to be heard. Cultivate the habit of listening, and it will really help your social skills.

Be interested in people's stories. Be open to learning something you did not know before from who's talking to you. Show interest in the story that person is telling you and be genuine about it. Know that interested people are always exciting, and you shouldn't be shy about asking people questions.

Don't complain all the time and don't be too negative. Do you ever wonder why we often avoid people who have no excellent vibes but prefer to deal with funny, cheerful, loving, and kind people? It's simply because the world is already filled with too many negativities and fear, and we can't afford to be plunged into another that can be avoided. If you're too negative and complain too much, you'll be repelling people away from you.

Remember people's names. One of the bad habits most people have is forgetting people's names. Such people who find it difficult to remember people's names all the time often hide under the facade of having "short memories," but remembering people's names is all about motivation and it's not really about your brainpower because there's a high chance that you'll recognize some people's name if you were paid a couple of dollars for it. What most people don't know is that people love it when their names are remembered, and therefore you should do whatever you have to do to remember. Ask people to spell their words out for you if it's hard, and don't be shy to repeat their names. Remember, you can never forget if you want to remember.

Remember people's stories. People actually find it thrilling to remember their stories because it means that you actually listened to them. As much as you can, remember what people are obsessed about, the details about the job, a side gig, hobbies, pets, or even the names of the family members. You can start or strengthen the casual friendship, spark new conversations, and set the foundation to follow up when you remember what people tell you.

Don't fill every gap with talking. You're having a conversation with someone, and you're the only one talking and talking all the time; no, things aren't done that way. Or, maybe the person has been speaking and saying different things, and you just kept mute; even when you can just nod your head to show you're in the conversation, you understand conversations are two-way streets.

Follow up. Following up is a marathon and not a sprint, and it's from there that relationships are built. The most authentic power of networking lies in following up. Considered rare and precious, people who follow-through are reliable, consistent, diligent, and caring.

Know when to leave. Conversations don't go on forever. Have a friendly discussion and move on.

Show love. Shower people with your love, help people, don't judge people, forgive people, see the best in people, compliment people, take an interest in what people are going through, admire people, respect people, love people! You may have all the social skills in this world, but it's all useless if you don't show love to people. Love is the ultimate social skill, and funny enough, it's the biggest trick of all social skills. Love is the key ingredient.

Reflection:
  - For each area of your life that you wish to be successful in, come up with some ideas of who can help you along the way.

➢ Then try to see how you can get in touch with them and
nurture a relationship with them.

Chapter 9: Secret 6– Your Time Is Sacred

The key is in not spending time but in investing it.–
Stephen R. Covey.

E veryone knows how valuable time is, and in this world, we're living in that everything is fast-paced, it's becoming increasingly difficult to keep up with changes and even maintain a schedule. And, this points to why one must be conscious of time management. Time management helps increase productivity and efficiency, and it is planning and organizing the time you plan to dedicate to your different activities. You'll be able to improve the use of time and save your valuable time when you practice time management and include your success rate at work and in life can be enhanced by effective time management. People who enjoy better productivity and engagement enable the correct use of time by exploring time management techniques to their advantage.

Time management skills are common traits of successful people, and if you want to walk on your path to achieving success, you must possess this skill, too. Aside from the skills of collaborating with others, negotiating deals, and communicating your ideas, time management is a skill that is vital for overall success, and luckily, it's a skill that's easy to learn. Still, it's pretty ironic that many care less about developing this skill because they feel it's not as crucial as other skills. Successful people can achieve many things in a year, while others take several years to do that same thing simply because of their time management skills.

Time management can help you get a promotion with a pay increase, deliver your projects successfully, and get ahead in your career. In a straightforward term, time management has to do with getting the right things done in less time because things will be easier for you, and you'll be able to achieve more when you become better at maintaining focus and managing your time.

Four D's of Time Management

You must follow the four Ds of effectiveness if you desire to have an effective time management schedule:

- **Desire**: You need to have the desire to understand the value of time if you want to be more effective at managing your time. Your confidence can get boosted when you acknowledge your desire to get better at managing your time.

- **Determination**: Most people fail at managing their time effectively because of the constant distractions they face, and for you to get rid of distractions, your deduction will play a significant role. Your time will get wasted when several distractions keep coming in your way during your essential tasks, and for you to get past this, you must channel your determination to get rid of them.

- **Decisiveness**: You can't stand on the fence to choose what's best for you. You know how crucial time management is for your success, and you have to decide to practice what will improve your life. Until it becomes a regular habit, keep practicing good time management practices, and let your sound sense of determination be constant.

- **Discipline**: Discipline is the fourth D. Everyone knows how vital the domain is. The environment determines if you're accurate about the decision, the determination, and your desire, and it's a step above all these steps combined. It takes discipline to do what you have to do. Even when you know what you should do, what you want to do, and what you've planned to do, it takes discipline to eventually do it. Domain helps you stay clear from getting involved in tasks that consume your time and efforts, and it also enables you to maintain the routine schedule you should follow.

Time is a Limited Resource

Time, when it's gone, it's gone forever. No one has the monopoly of time; you can't buy time to get more of it. When we refuse to do whatever we should, we can't get that time again once the time comes and goes. Though you may do that thing later, that time you've lost can't be regained. Time cannot be saved (it's not your money that you can put in your savings account), time is perishable (it doesn't last long), and it's the most valuable thing one can have (time is a decisive determinant factor of success) — time is man's most precious resource. We all have the same time; 86,400 seconds, 1,440 minutes, and 24 hours in a day, and how we use our time and what we use our time on are significant factors that determine how our life will turn out. It's high time you started putting things in a new perspective because time management means everything. Network, catch up with an old friend, learn a new skill, read, or exercise, instead of spending the whole day watching Netflix. You'll cherish every second of time once you realize that time is a finite resource.

Why Time Management is Important

Reduces Stress. Time management makes you less stressed and more relaxed in the long run because it makes you more prepared to efficiently handle whatever life throws your way. You'll be able to prevent last-minute surprises, meet deadlines, and feel more in control when you manage your time more wisely. Time management and stress management go hand in hand. We all know how stress can be dangerous to one's health. And, if you're not aware of the dangers or complications stress can cause, take note that stress can cause some to commit suicide, reduce your immunity and ability to heal, cause blood sugar imbalances, suppress your thyroid, and affect your brain as well. Cirrhosis of the liver, lung ailments, cancer, and heart disease are also some of the health illnesses that have been associated with chronic stress.

You Accomplish More With Less Effort. You'll be able to breeze through your tasks more quickly when you don't lose momentum, and you're conscious of what needs to get done because of your time management skill. Eventually, you'll become more productive, get distractions eliminated, and improve your ability to focus when you take control of your time.

Less Re-work. You have a high chance of making severe errors and forgetting an essential item when you're flawed with time. You won't make as many mistakes, and you realize that you'll be able to stay focused, become more organized, and be encouraged to work more efficiently when you practice time management. And, since you won't forget to add your tasks to your to-do list, you won't have to struggle or lament over redoing a study, even though the study may not be perfect.

Small Steps Lead to Big Goals. You'll have to take several steps before you can reach the top, and time management will help you maintain your focus on these steps. You'll need to take one action at a time for you to reach the top — you can think of it as a set of stairs. You'll have to take some baby steps to achieve your goals, and even though you cannot perform these goals overnight, your time management will help you greatly in achieving success. Remember that you won't have time for the big things if you don't have time for the small stuff.

Identifies Your Top Priorities. Time management helps you focus on doing tasks that are the most urgent and very important because it propels you to prioritize, and this is indubitably one of its most significant influences.

Improves Decision Making. You'll get to make the best decision possible when you analyze the information with you, reflect, and enjoyably sit back doing these when you're not pressured for time. Most people make a wrong decision because they have an essential decision but have no time to think through the information.

Eliminates Wasted Time. It's easy for you to be one step ahead and jump right into the next task when practicing effective time management. The simple thing is that you won't have to waste your precious time pondering on what to do next when you know what you have to do.

Boosts Your Reputation. If you're so flaky and unreliable, you're presenting yourself as someone who can't be trusted with a project. Imagine you missing deadlines or showing up late every time to a meeting. Do you think this will make you successful? You'll be able to follow through on what you promised to do, meet a deadline, and show up constantly when you practice time management.

Gives You More Free Time. You'll be able to have more leisure time and make the most of your hours when you manage your time effectively. You reap the benefit of getting more hours in a day when you order your time better.

Must-have Time Management Skills

Organization. Being well-organized means you're taking detailed, diligent notes, you have a tidy environment, you're able to quickly locate certain documents, and you can maintain an up-to-date calendar. You'll have a clearer picture of when and what you need to complete when you stay organized.

Prioritization. A vital key to being an excellent time manager is assessing each of your responsibilities for priority. For prioritization, there's no particular way to go. You may choose to start with the most time-sensitive, then proceed to the simpler ones.

Goal-setting. You'll enjoy success in your career when you set both short- and long-term goals. When you practice goal setting, you'll be fully conscious of what you need to prioritize to accomplish your goal and clearly understand your end goal. To become an excellent time manager, setting goals is the first step you must take.

Communication. You'll be able to delegate and improve the clarity of your goals and plans to people you work with when you develop strong communication skills.

Planning. You'll be able to stick to your schedule and accomplish things when you efficiently plan out your day. Take note that planning is a fundamental part of time management.

Delegation. If you are managing a project, you can as well practice delegating tasks. This skill is most often done by managers. Take note that it's only when your company accomplishes goals and you finish the work you have at hand that you'll be called an excellent time manager. To manage your time well and eventually achieve your goals, you must also practice having boundaries.

Stress management. To perform well when going through your schedule and staying motivated, you need to positively handle stress. You must be attentive to your mental health, even while you're practicing good time management. As you accomplish tasks, you can reward yourself in small ways or include minor breaks to relieve yourself from stress throughout your day.

9 Types of Time Management Techniques

1. Pareto Analysis (a.k.a., the 80/20 rule). You'll be able to prioritize tasks that are most effective to solve problems when you use this technique. This technique affirms that 80 percent of our outcomes come from 20 percent of our actions. And, the Italian economist Vilfredo Pareto is the one who created this 80/20 rule.

How does it work?

- Maybe your grades are dropping, or you're facing other challenges. Just list some problems you're facing.
- Get to know what the root cause of the problem is. As you dig deeper, you may get to realize that social media has been sapping most of your time, and that's why your grades are slipping.

- If you have more significant problems, assign higher numbers to them, but at this stage, the idea is to set a score for each situation.
- Problems caused by excessive time wasted on social media can be grouped together; just group problems together by cause.
- Now, the first issue you would work on is the group with the highest score, and for you to arrive at this, you'll have to add up the score of each group.
- Take action.

This Pareto Analysis, which is also known as the 80/20 rule, benefits two kinds of people:

- Analytical thinkers
- Problem solvers

2. Pomodoro Technique. Breaking down your work at intervals with a timer is what this technique uses. The entrepreneur and author Francesco Cirillo is the genius behind the creation of the Pomodoro Technique. Named after the tomato-shaped timer crated by Francesco, each interval is known as a Pomodoro. This technique is best suitable for those who feel burned out from work/school and creative thinkers. And, it entails using a timer to focus on a task and getting breaks in-between, just to give your brain a break.

3. Eisenhower Matrix. Critical thinkers and people in leadership positions are the two kinds of people that benefit significantly from the Eisenhower Matrix technique. Also referred to as the urgent-important matrix and invented by Dwight Eisenhower, this technique focuses on sorting tasks into urgent vs. not urgent vs. unimportant. Basically, it involves organizing your tasks into four distinct quadrants.

4. Time Blocking Method. Time blocking is one tool for productive, successful people. And Elon Musk is regarded as being the inventor of this technique. From studying for a test to eating breakfast and a host of other tasks, you may have, assigning each time block in your day to a lesson from the moment you wake up is what this technique entails. Analytical thinkers, working students, and parents are the kinds of people that benefit from using these techniques.

6. Getting Things Done (GTD) Method. People who feel overwhelmed in their daily lives and struggle to focus on one thing at a time are the two kinds of people who benefit immensely from using this technique. Taking actionable work items by breaking down your tasks after getting them recorded on paper is what this technique entails. Author David Allen created the getting things by strategy. To apply this technique, all you have to do is conscious of the actions that have your attention, clarify them, organize your efforts by making a priority list, reflect and take a review, and then get engaged.

6. Rapid Planning Method (RPM). People who have long-term goals, working students, and parents are the kinds of people that stand to benefit more this technique. Developed to focus on a vision and train the brain, motivational speaker Tony Robbins is the genius behind this technique. "Result, purpose, and massive action plan" or "rapid planning method" is what "RPM" stands for.

7. Pickle Jar Theory. Concrete thinkers and visual people are the two kinds of people that will benefit immensely from this technique. This theory allows you to set priorities for your day and plan tasks with time to spare because it helps you identify the things that are not useful in your everyday life and the valuable things. Let's say you have rocks, pebbles, and sand, all contained in a pickle jar to the brim, and while the stones sit at the top, the sand is at the bottom. The most important tasks that need to get done today are the rocks. The pebbles are the pebbles or activities that can be done on another day or by someone else but need to be completed.

Social media, emails, text messages, phone calls, and other disrupting elements of your day are what the sand represents. With this illustration, you'll have to look at your tasks and think of how they relate to this theory. Write out your activities that are rocks, pebbles, and sands, but it's often advisable that you start from the least important to the most important (sands — rocks) and be very honest. With this, you'll have a clearer picture of what you should focus on and do later or what shouldn't waste your time.

8. Eat That Frog Technique. People with long-term goals and abstract thinkers are the two kinds of people that will benefit from this technique. This technique simply has to do with starting your day by first tackling the most challenging tasks. Nothing worse will happen to you for the rest of the day when you eat a live frog the first thing in the morning — those are the words of Mark Twain, and it's no surprise that this technique is named after him. As you intend to implement this technique, ask yourself, what do you need to do today? Write them down in order of priority and start "eating your frogs." Make sure you eat the nastiest one first if you've got over one frog on your plate.

Valuable Tips for Time Management

Set goals the right way. To see things through, use the SMART goal setting method. You'll be forced to fall off track if you don't set your goals the right way.

The acronym SMART stands for;

- S — Specific

- M — Meaningful
- A — Achievable
- R — Relevant
- T — Time-based

Audit your time for seven days straight. Record your assessment in a journal or on your phone as you keep asking yourself what you're doing. Assess how you spend the time you have presently and spend seven days straight doing that.

Spend your mornings on MITs. You'll enjoy having a tremendous momentum that will aid you to sail through the rest of the day when you accomplish your most important tasks (MITs) of the day.

Schedule email response times. Take note that someone will call or text you if there's something urgent. You should schedule a time to read and respond to emails because it's easy to get distracted when your email is pouring in. Throughout the day, turn off your email.

Turn off social media app alerts. You'll be able to focus on the task at hand and even have some peace of mind when you do this.

Declutter and organize. Declutter and manage if you want to avoid losing focus. Take note you lose time when you lose focus, and studies have proven that our environment helps us gain or lose focus.

Eliminate bad habits. Several habits steal our precious time; it could go out frequently to drink with friends, playing games, excessively surfing social media, or Netflix binge-watching. Our bad habits are one of our biggest time-wasters, and if you're serious about achieving big goals in life, you must learn to eliminate your bad habits to use your time wisely.

Habits to Practice

1. Delegate Tasks. Managing your tasks properly is what delegation means, and you shouldn't think it's about running away or shying away from your responsibilities. You risk stress and burnout when you want to take on more tasks than you should.

2. Prioritize Work. Beware of unimportant tasks because "these guys" appear less stressful or way more manageable, but they have a way of making us waste too much of our energy on them, and, of course, they enjoy consuming much of our precious time. Do well to make a list of tasks that require your immediate attention before you start the day. In an order that works for you and your schedule, you'll be able to get things done, and you'll also be conscious of where to put your energy.

To boost and foster productivity, you must identify urgent tasks that require completion and priority.

3. Create a Schedule. You'll get motivated, and you'll also enjoy having a sense of accomplishment when you're able to check some items off your list as you complete them. Make sure your tasks are attainable. Focus on the essentials and prioritize your tasks as you create your 'To Do' list.

4. Set up Deadlines. To get a visual cue on your tasks, put your deadline near your workspace or write it on a sticky note. Stick to your deadline and make sure you set a realistic one once you have a task at hand. You may even reward yourself for meeting a difficult challenge if you challenge yourself to meet the deadline.

5. Overcome Procrastination. When we feel bored or overwhelmed, we have the tendency to procrastinate. Procrastination can gravely impact your personal life and career, and you could end up wasting essential time and energy. However, you can stay more on track when you break up the more arduous tasks throughout the day by scheduling more minor, fun activities.

6. Deal With Stress Wisely. Stress comes in various forms for different people, and when you accept more than you can accomplish, you make yourself vulnerable to stress. For lowering your stress response. The key is to find what works for you. And, it could listen to music or a podcast, taking part in your favorite hobby, calling up a friend, practicing meditation, exercising, or getting outside. However, you may try a couple of breathing techniques if you don't have time for anything else.

7. Avoid Multitasking. To improve time management skills, make sure you avoid multitasking because it hampers productivity. When you focus and concentrate on one thing, you'll see that you'll do better. Note that an efficient way of getting things done isn't by multitasking. Don't be deceived.

8. Start Early. You'll be more clear-headed, creative, and calmer when you get up early. You'll even have more time to plan your day, think, and relax later when you start your day early. One of the everyday things successful people have is that they get up early. Take note that your focus, motivation, and productivity get affected when your energy levels start going down, which happens naturally as the day progresses.

9. Take Regular Breaks. Your productivity can be affected, and your body can also suffer some consequences when you're too stressed. Do well to take a break for 10 to 15 minutes if you're feeling tired and stressed. You can even spend time with your friends and family and take a break from work altogether. Or perhaps do some quick stretches, listen to some music, or take a walk. You'll be able to get back to work with energy again later and feel relaxed when you schedule your break times.

10. Learn to say No. A great way to take care of yourself and your time is by saying no, and this doesn't mean that you're selfish. Before you agree to take on extra work, do well to look at your to-do list. If you're already bombarded with so much to do, politely refuse to accept additional tasks.

Reflection:
- ➤ Look at your schedule and see what you are spending most of your time on
- ➤ Are there activities you want or think you should do more of?
- ➤ Are there things you want to do less of or erase?
- ➤ How can you adjust your schedule to reflect on what's important to you?

Chapter 10: Secret 7– Helping Others Helps You

Help others achieve their dreams, and you will achieve yours. - Les Brown

H happiness is found in helping others, and it's no surprise that the most significant thinkers have always emphasized how important it is to extend a helping hand to one another. Help somebody if you want happiness for a lifetime. A secret to living a more meaningful, productive, wealthier, healthier, and happier life is by helping others. Altruism is pleasurable, and it's hard-wired in the brain — experiments have shown evidence to prove this. Undoubtedly, giving is a powerful pathway to lasting happiness and personal growth. And, as humans, we all rely on the people around us for emotional support during good and bad times, for we have a strong tendency to reach out to someone when something terrible happens, when we have something important to share, or when we receive surprising news. And, because of this sense of connection in us, it becomes vital for us to be there for people because these same people will also be there for us when we need their support. Take note that what you give and not what you get helps you discover the real meaning of life, and finding a passionate relationship, following a specific blueprint for your life, or stacking up material possessions isn't what defines true fulfillment. Giving is the secret to living, and we need to give back to the community.

Scientific Benefits of Helping Others

Lending a hand to those in need has proven beneficial, and studies have affirmed that we can get our sense of well-being, health, and happiness boosted when we give back to the community. You're making yourself better when you volunteer your energy, time, and money to assist others, and this as well goes a long way to make the world a better place for everyone and the generations that are coming.

1. Helping others can help you live longer. Some factors that can significantly and positively affect your long-term health can get fostered when you practice the act of giving. Volunteering allows us to enhance our social lives, and it's also proven to be a great way to ease loneliness. More so, it helps to increase one's sense of life satisfaction, reducing the rates of depression, staving off diseases, and improving the ability to manage stress. Your health can be improved in ways that can lengthen your lifespan when you partake in activities that help you give back.

2. Altruism is contagious. When you do good to others, you're encouraging multitudes of people to do likewise. Dozens of people can be inspired to make a difference when you give back to the community. You can cause a chain reaction of other altruistic acts when you perform a good deed. The person you're helping, whose life will be transformed, will also find it purposeful to impact the lives of other people, and this will just keep going on and on like a chain link.

3. Helping others makes us happy. If you're sad and you feel immersed in despondency, help someone. We enjoy a neurochemical sense of reward with the mental boost we get when we give back to others. Researchers have as well proven that our sense of well-being gets heightened when we volunteer.

4. Helping others may help with chronic pain. There's a strong possibility that you'll experience a reduction in your pain symptoms when you try to volunteer. A study has affirmed this.

5. Helping others lowers blood pressure. You can release yourself from the shackles of loneliness and the stress that usually comes with it when you volunteer.

6. Helping others promotes positive behaviors in teens. Several teenagers who enjoy a better self-image do volunteer — this is under sociologists.

7. Helping others gives us a sense of purpose and satisfaction. Your overall sense of purpose and identity can be enhanced by volunteering. If you're seeking more meaning in your everyday existence, you might volunteer.

Why You Should Give Back to the Community

Both you and your community stand to benefit immensely when you give back. You can better the lives of people elsewhere in the world, the people in your community, your loved ones, and that of everyone around you basically when you give back. The significance of giving back to society cannot be underrated.

Improves mental health. You'll feel good in both the short and long term with the happy chemicals induced as rewards by the brain when you volunteer. Research has proven that psychological distresses like depression can be decreased, and we can increase happiness by volunteering.

Improves physical health. Among several other health benefits, you stand to enjoy decreased mortality risk and lower risk for hypertension when you volunteer. Your physical health does benefit immensely when you volunteer and, if you desire to live longer, embrace the act of volunteering. Combining building homes, stocking a food pantry, or other likewise physical activities with volunteering offers more health benefits.

Expands your network. You never know who you'll meet when you volunteer, and volunteering is more like a networking opportunity. The chances are high that you'll meet like-minded people when you volunteer, and don't forget that the key to achieving your dreams is surrounding yourself with good people.

Develops new skills. Volunteering offers an opportunity for growth. It helps you meet new people and propels you to get out of your comfort zone. You also stand to gain soft skills like public speaking when you get involved and remember that if you're not growing, you're dying.

Transforms your perspective. You'll be able to see how much you have to be grateful for when you help others. Giving back to the community helps change your mindset, and it's a great way to adopt an attitude of gratitude.

Fulfills your most profound human needs. You'll feel helpful, unique, and needed when your needs for contribution and significance get fulfilled by volunteering. One of the best ways to fulfill our deepest human needs is by giving back to society, and we get to innately realize the significance when we contribute to the community.

How to Give Back to the Community

There are several ways to make you're living in a happier and more loving place, and you can positively impact your hometown, whether you're donating money to someone in need or volunteering at your local food bank. You can make a real difference with any small or big action to give back to the community. And, for you to connect more deeply with yourself and with those around you, there are some strategies you can make use of, and here are some of them;

1. Find your purpose. You'll get closer to achieving your personal goals, have a feeling like you're making a significant difference for a good cause, and reach a greater sense of fulfillment when you work towards your purpose by giving back to the community. Our actions are often driven by a more significant meaning, and purpose is the backbone of giving back to society. Ask yourself; what is it in life that goes you?

2. Start small and start today. Helping your community isn't about how much you have but how devoted you choose to be to play a part in the lives of others and also developing a mindset that contributes. The chances are high that if you become wildly successful, you won't give back to your community if you don't give back when you have just been so tiny. You can always start today, no matter what resources you have. Stop waiting to give back. Not giving back is about a lack of resourcefulness, and it isn't about a lack of resources. There are several easy you can start giving back to the community. You may donate a portion of your paychecks if you make a reasonable sum as income, or you could even donate your time to volunteering at a local community center.

3. Create a ripple effect. A great way to give back to the community is by creating a ripple effect. Imagine you serving as a source of inspiration that encourages many people to give back to their community? Do you know the level of good you'll be doing to your community with that? The number of minds you'll inspire by your actions to follow your steps? Over $45 billion has been given to charity by the Bill and Melinda Gates Foundation. Do you know how many people's lives these two individuals have impacted across different parts of the world? People like Serena Williams, Marc Benioff, Oprah Winfrey, and Bill Gates are some of the few people that come to mind when one thinks of some of the most admired people in the world. And, these people prioritize giving back to society, dedicate themselves to creating value in the lives of others, and keep spreading the gospel of charity diligently. Your contributions can inspire others, too, even if you can't contribute as much as Bill Gates does. You'll also encourage others to get involved with your positive actions once you give back to the community. Others will be inspired by you to do the same, for you'll be creating a ripple of positive impact when you understand the significance of giving back to the community.

4. Find what fits. To give back to the community, find what works. If you want to contribute to society without stretching yourself too thin, go for opportunities along with your lifestyle and ideals. You may consider financial or in-kind donations if you're low on time, use your network to facilitate others' contributions or donate your time if you're on a limited budget, help beautify local parks and waterways if you love gardening, give back to your community's schools if you love children. Whatever area of philanthropy that speaks to you, just follow through with it. Take the time to find what works and find a fit between what interests you and how you can meet a need; this giving back is all about. In fact, you can do a lot of good in giving back to the community by just visiting an elderly neighbor, recycling, or engaging in any act of inexpensive and small kindness.

5. Embrace your life as a resource. To embrace everything you offer, all you need is self-acceptance, because you don't have to be perfect to give back. No one can duplicate your perspective and skills because of the set of experiences you're equipped with — everyone's life experience is unique. Don't let your limiting beliefs make you feel like giving is a feat that's reserved for heroes alone, no. You'll feel more natural to offer when you contribute small and progress the habit of giving back. You'll also gain physical and mental health benefits and find a personal sense of joy and fulfillment. Understand that you're a resource to your community and the world at large, and in making the world a better place, you shouldn't draw back because your community needs you!

Here are more explicit ideas on how to give back to your community;

- **Find the Right Cause For You** — Get connected with a cause that you are passionate about.
- **Spread Good News** — In a world so often inundated with the bad, commit yourself to give the gift of good news.
- **Donate to Holiday Food Drives** — Support community centers, schools, grocery stores, and businesses organizing food drives.
- **Support Your Local Farmers** — You can support their business by buying just a little of fresh produce from them, even though you may not do all your grocery shopping there. Shop at your local farmers' market or farm stands and support the diligent farmers in your community.
- **Donate Blood** — You can help in saving lives during a medical emergency or medical procedures.
- **Become a Volunteer Firefighter** — A physical test, training hours, and an EMT certification are often required to volunteer for a local fire department.

However, based on the location and the department, there may be a slight variance.

- **Set up a Collection Jar** — You'll be giving back to a local charity you want to support when creating a collection box.

- **Become a Girl or Boy Scout Leader** — You can use this opportunity to provide mentorship opportunities to the youth in your community and teach young girls and boys survival skills.

- **Join a Community Garden** — You can grow fresh produce for the community and teach a new skill to others by taking up a plot at your community garden and putting that green thumb to good use.

- **Build a Home for Someone in Need** — You can donate housewares such as appliances and furniture to organizations seeking hands-on help from volunteers. Help to build a roof over the heads of disadvantaged residents.

- **Volunteer at Your Local Senior Center** — You can help the aging residents feel connected to their community by doing simple acts like joining in on a game of chess, playing music, reading stories, or dropping by to say hello.

- **Become a Big Brother or Big Sister** — You can help create a more connected community and help to change the lives of youth in search of a role model when you volunteer with a community-based mentorship program.

- **Organize a Community Clean-up** — Your neighbors and the environment will thank you when you help make the area more welcoming, paint park benches, pull weeds, and gather litter. The local park is a usual gathering spot for communities.

- **Sponsor a Youth Sports Team** — You can give back to the teams in your community and even get the name of your business out there when you ensure a youth sports team gets the equipment they need and subsidizes costs.

- **Share Your Pet With Others** — Arrange a visit to your local hospital, veterans club, and senior center and share your well-trained pet with your community. You can foster social interactions among people, decrease loneliness and depression, reduce stress, and improve human cardiovascular health with human-animal interaction — this is following a study on The Health Benefits of Companion Animals.

- **Schedule a Volunteer Day With Your Colleagues** — If you've been looking for a way to give to the community that has been helping the growth of your business and even boosts office morale, a month, or annual volunteer day for your office. As a business owner, you may even permit your employees to take a personal day to volunteer or have a corporate affiliation with a nonprofit.

- **Donate Your Workwear** — Give it a second life and a new home instead of just throwing them out.

- **Donate to a Charity** — Donations are often tax deductible, and every dollar counts to help those in need, big or small. To donate to your favorite charity, set aside a portion of your income.

- **Help Those in Need Abroad** — Help children in conflict zones build schools or just find a charity abroad that can use your support. Understand that there's life beyond your city, town, or neighborhood, and these people that are beyond the reach of your geographic boundaries are a part of your community too.

How Giving Back Contributes to Your Success and Career

1. Meet New People. You enjoy more engaging social activities and get rewarded with better friendships when you give out your time to your local community. You also want the opportunity of being invited to social events, make new friends, and even expand your social network. Getting involved in a good cause in your community is very beneficial for your success because it can plug you into a network of people that can help you when times are complex, and it can also help build your interpersonal skills and self-confidence.

2. Realize Your Potential. Giving makes you more prosperous and improves your effectiveness because it furnishes you with some new skills that you can take into your field and even opens you up to a new career. You'll keep wanting to do good and have an impetus to keep going when you help others and see how valuable it is added. Muhammad Ali once said that the rent we pay for our rooms here on earth is our service to others. And this is super true.

3. You Will Learn New Things. Volunteering will continually improve you as a person, whether you're providing support with your existing skills or you're just involved in empathy for fellow humans. You'll be taught new things when you do some work directly within the community or give back to the community by helping local businesses. Doing good within your local community can help you improve yourself. It's a win-win. Know that no matter what stage you are at in life, there's always something that can be improved upon because no one is super perfect.

4. Balance. You'll be more successful in other areas of your life when you help create happiness and contribute some of your time to the betterment of others by maintaining balance in your life. When you permit yourself to contribute to the lives of others, you'll be able to find true happiness. If you want to be happy, don't be egocentric. Ensure you do things for yourself but also for others. Striking a balance is the key to happiness in life.

5. Responsibility. Volunteering in the local community can foster your sense of responsibility. Several people will be reliant on you for survival when you're committed, and the understanding and skills you get from this experience can be helpful later and prepare you for personal and professional success.

6. Influences New Career Ideas. You can get an idea of what voids need to be filled and what's missing; whether you're going out to get your hands dirty in your community, speaking on a panel about careers to students, educating youths on the significance of following their dreams, or helping raise money for a charity event. You'll become relatively closer to closing a gap in your community and be propelled to discover new career ideas and business ventures by the inspiration you get from your volunteering experiences.

7. Allows You to be a Mentor. You'll be able to show the ropes of the game in your fields to young minds, and you'll also come across young professionals who will need your guidance when you help others.

8. Motivate Others. Giving back to the community is vital for organizations that want to enjoy more success. Your employees will become more motivated and inspired when you embrace the idea of giving back to the community. Giving back makes people feel good, and many people love to do it. And it's conducive to your organization.

Ways to Give Back as an Entrepreneur

You can help advance a social cause with your entrepreneurial skills and experience, from finding innovative social impact solutions to contributing to sustainable development goals. Philanthropy options are endless; whether you want to make monetary donations to charitable causes or volunteer your time, there are several ways you can give back as an entrepreneur.

Practicing philanthropic entrepreneur is very important because you get to enjoy these four benefits of giving;

- How It Makes You Feel: You'll get to see with a different perspective, get a boost in your self-esteem, and feel good when you practice true selfless philanthropy.
- Skill-Building: You'll be able to build many new skills when you give your time to a unique organization such as the Habitat for Humanity (you'll get to learn how to

build a house or, better still, have a better idea and insight on how home construction works.

- Networking: You'll be able to meet new people to forge relationships with when you give back as time.

- Karma: The more you give, the more you get. Many entrepreneurs believe in this. Those who give back often get blessings from the forces of nature.

Here are some ways you can give back as an entrepreneur;

1. Give Back With Money or Time. This is an easy way to give back as an entrepreneur. Teaching your craft is an easy way to give back. You'll be able to cause a spark in someone else's entrepreneurial endeavors or help some people with a source of financial freedom with the skill you teach. Assisting people to learn a new, valuable skill for free is a fantastic thing to do, and you should feel relaxed discussing what you are an expert in. Sharing what you're passionate about with others is something you probably would enjoy doing. You can see the value of your philanthropy firsthand and make a big difference in any community with donations, such as sponsoring a community youth program or a new park project. Make your donation local, and your first stop for monetary philanthropy could be personal and professional growth and success.

2. Raise Money For A Foundation Or Charity. Raising money is a great way to amplify your generosity. Of course, a foundation or a charity can not reject a monetary gift, and it's also a great idea to write a check, but if you want to do more, explore the advantages of your strong network or database for philanthropic purposes.

4. Volunteer at a School or Children's Hospital. Regardless of any amount of money you may have to donate, know that what's far more important to kids in need is your time, and your priority should give your time. Any institution where children are in need, a school, or a children's cancer clinic is a fine place where you can volunteer your time. Your philanthropist will have a long-lasting effect if it involves children and connecting in fun ways with children in need is a great idea, especially if you're an entrepreneur that's young at heart.

5. **Give a Local Business a Boost**. Whether you have a knack for finding financial means or you're a social media marketing whiz, taking your awesome entrepreneurial nuggets to a local business can be a great way to give back. Entrepreneurs often know how to build a business with earning potential, market themselves, build industry relationships, convince investors, land, seed money, and are very crafty in their field and

passionate about what they do. And resources can help a small local business.

Habits to Practice

1. Be there for people in their moments of vulnerability. Be there for someone who really needs you whenever you get the chance to be.

2. Personalize. You'll get more chances to connect, engage, and be prompted to help when you personalize.

3. Lookout for others' blindsides. Inform people whenever you come across something that could benefit them.

4. End conversations by asking how you can be helpful. When you know what's truly helpful to other people, there's a possibility of you being motivated to take a step to help.

5. Practice recognizing people. If you're working with someone who's putting in a lot of effort, identify the person's actions. Praise people when you should, and acknowledge their efforts.

6. Give selfless feedback. Be "available" to give feedback that will help people become better rather than just trying to show off and display your authority on a subject.

8. **Write meaningful things**. You have a splendid chance of doing something meaningful to someone with the information you write

Reflection:

➤ Reflect on some questions about how you can give back
  ○ What are you leaving behind?
  ○ What purpose does the money you're making serve beyond paying the bills?
  ○ What matters to you?
➤ Make a clear list on paper of causes you are interested in or care about. Research them and find some organizations or people to support.
  ○ This could be by becoming an advisor, sharing your skills and expertise, becoming an advocate for the cause, or simply contributing some money.

Final Thoughts

We all desire to grow, improve, and ultimately achieve success, whether starting our own business, speed reading, learning a new musical instrument like the guitar, or losing weight. And it may appear like achieving success is elusive when we keep trying and falling. However, success isn't an illusion, and it's pretty much achievable. If you're close to successful people, have been in contact with any, or probably read about a few, you'll notice that there are two everyday things about successful people. Foremost, they work on their mindset because they're conscious of how their mood can significantly affect their success chances. And second, they develop certain helpful habits that propel them towards the realization of their goals.

The quality of the habits you form determines what you'll ever accomplish and who you'll be. Habits determine 95% of a person's behavior, and the common difference between successful and unsuccessful people is their habits. Your habits can affect the trajectory of your life. Habits can either be the horse you ride on to develop a life of failure and mediocrity or be the propelling factor that aids your success. Occurring in our day-to-day routine, habits are consistent behavioral patterns, and the beautiful thing about them is that they can help us live a prosperous life and become successful when we create good habits and adopt positive behavior.

Habits are the foundation of life, and for you to achieve success, you must desist from practicing harmful habits that can keep you from accomplishing your goal and ultimately achieving success, but stick to developing good habits and emulate the characteristics of successful people. More so, it's also essential that you're conscious of the 7 secrets to success that I have mentioned in this book. What are the seven secrets again? Let me brush you up on this quickly once again. Foremost, developing a growth mindset is very important because it can determine how you face adversity, drive you, help you gain perspective, and affect your self-esteem. Second, set goals and be conscious of what you're working towards — this is very important because it will offer you a benchmark for determining your success, and it will also help you take control of your life's direction.

Consistency is the third secret because it will help you progress over time and create stability. The fourth secret is developing solution-based thinking and learning to be creative, as this will help you confront obstacles, no matter how high or small they are, rather than compromising and throwing in the towel. Building social skills will be helpful in dealing with people from different walks of life. The sixth secret is learning how to manage time effectively, and this is very important because it will boost your reputation, give you more free time, make you enjoy less re-work, help you achieve work-life balance, avoid feeling overwhelmed, and reduce stress. The last secret which caps all the seven secrets is given. Giving back contributes to your success, and giving is like you pointing a finger towards someone with your other four fingers indirectly pointing back at you! Just as the golden rule says, do unto others what you want to be done unto you!

Success is not accidental. No. It isn't. And you don't have to look a certain way, go to an Ivy League school, or come from a wealthy family before you can achieve success. Regardless of who you are or whatever your background is, there are some things you can do to become successful, and thankfully, I've already explored these things in this book, and it's up to you to put them into use and make them work for you.

Remember that you can always enhance your life in ways you never imagined when you adopt the right approach and you should never for once doubt your ability to succeed because if you believe, you can achieve! So, adopt a can-do mindset and brace up yourself to work on the tips that have been outlined in this book and apply them to the real-life situations you encounter.

I'll also be looking forward to reading your reviews so, do well to drop them and don't hold back on sharing your thoughts about the book.

Thank you!

About The Author

Randy Wagner is a financial investor, entrepreneur, sales, marketing, and technology expert. Randy Wagner has also become a successful entrepreneur and a nonfiction author. He serves as the CEO of a private company. Randy Wagner earned a Master's Degree in Psychology from Columbia University. He was born in New York City. Randy Wagner has extensive experience with financial independence. He noticed changes in his quality of life as time passed. It is important to note that my habits have played a significant role in my success. Habits play a vital role in your personality and energy, which affects your life's outcome.

To prepare for his career as an entrepreneur, Randy Wagner supplied coffee to private and public organizations as a source of income. I could improve my financial situation by selling coffee. Passive income is an excellent way to increase your wealth. Throughout my life, I have developed passive income through the methods I have applied. The activities required beforehand, and the training needed may, however, vary between all of them. This can have implications for your level of passiveness. I became more optimistic about life as time passed, my confidence increased, and I could pay my bills and provide for my parents and siblings. All of us graduated from college. My siblings are consultants for organizations, and I am a mental health therapist, expert entrepreneur and professional writer. All I had to do was step up to become the CEO (Chief Executive Officer) of a company called me, with the sole purpose of winning more and losing less in everything I engaged in. By helping others with their challenges and adversities, I have learned a great deal about how to overcome obstacles and move forward in life. My goal is to encourage you to create original works, explore new ideas, and challenge yourself.

Recommended Reading Books

Passive Income Strategies to Build Your Wealth: Create Stability, Security, and Freedom in Your Financial Life, Second Edition. By Randy Wagner.

Success Multiplied: How to Multiply Your Business 10X, Live the Fastest Way Humanly Possible & Live a Regret-Free Life. By Randy Wagner.

References

Erin Marie. (November 2, 2016) Change Habits to Transform Your Life. http://www.healthhappensathome.com/blog/2016/8/19/change-habits-to-transform-life-a-success-story

Martin, Luenendonk (October 5, 2019) How Your Habits Can Help Determine Your Success and Potential. https://www.cleverism.com/how-your-habits-determine-success-and-potential/

Chris Spark. (February 19, 2016) Why Habits Are More Important Than We Imagine. https://medium.com/@ForcingFunction/why-habits-are-more-important-than-we-can-imagine-d44628036117

Ali Montag (September 15, 2018) This is Billionaire Jeff Bezos's Daily Routines And Its Sets Him For Success. https://www.cnbc.com/2018/09/14/billionaire-jeff-bezos-shares-the-daily-routine-he-uses-to-succeed.html

Insider (March 15, 2015) A CEO shares 3-hours morning routine that sets him up for success. https://www.businessinsider.com/gary-vaynerchuks-morning-routine-2015-3?r=US&IR=T

Lindsay Tigar (September 6, 2018) 5 Daily Habits to Steal from Oprah Winfrey, Including Working Out Every

Single Day. https://www.goalcast.com/2018/09/06/5-daily-habits-to-steal-from-oprah-winfrey/

Habitify Blog (n. d) Why Habits are Important for Success. https://www.habitify.me/blog/why-habits-are-important-for-success

Jessica Agyekum (n. d) 7 Things That Will Prevent You From Being Successful. https://www.lifehack.org/323869/7-things-that-will-prevent-you-from-being-successful

J.B. Glossinger (Feb 7, 2017) 4 horrible habits keeping you from success. https://www.bizjournals.com/bizjournals/how-to/growth-strategies/2017/02/4-horrible-habits-keeping-you-from-success.html

James Clear (n. d) How to Break a Bad Habit and Replace It With a Good One. https://jamesclear.com/how-to-break-a-bad-habit

Cassie Shortsleeve (August 28, 2018) 5 Science-Approved Ways to Break a Bad Habit. https://time.com/5373528/break-bad-habit-science/

Crystal Raypole (October 29, 2019). How to Break a Habit (and Make It Stick) https://www.healthline.com/health/how-to-break-a-habit

Lolly Daskal (n. d) Top 10 Qualities of Highly Successful People. https://www.lollydaskal.com/leadership/top-10-qualities-highly-successful-people/

Shyam Ramanathan (n. d) 11 Traits of Highly Successful
People. https://thriveglobal.com/stories/11-traits-of-
highly-successful-people/

Dan Schawbel (December 17, 2013) 14 Things Every
Successful Person Has In Common.
https://www.forbes.com/sites/danschawbel/2013/12/1
7/14-things-every-successful-person-has-in-
common/?sh=6f9147893c74

Lindsay Racen (December 21, 2016) 5 things the world's most
successful people have in common.
https://www.brandman.edu/news-and-events/blog/5-
things-the-worlds-most-successful-people-have-in-
common

Timothy Sykes (June 20, 2018) 5 Traits of Successful People.
https://www.entrepreneur.com/article/315161

Keshav Bhatt (November 27,2020) The Secret of Success to
Achieving Anything You Want Revealed.
https://www.lifehack.org/805803/becoming-
successful

Mind Tools (n. d) Golden Rule of Goal Setting Five Rules to
Set Yourself Up for Success.
https://www.mindtools.com/pages/article/newHTE_9
0.htm

Delan Cooper (Nov 25, 2018) How Giving Back to the
Community Contributes to Your Own Success.
https://addicted2success.com/life/how-giving-back-
to-the-community-contributes-to-your-own-success/

Vincent Carlos (June 1, 2017) No One Succeeds Alone: Why Einstein, Aristotle And Disney All Had Mentors. https://www.linkedin.com/pulse/want-mentored-warren-buffett-spend-20-bookstore-vincent-carlos

Joshua becker (n. d) Why Helping Others Succeed Can Be Your Greatest Success. https://www.becomingminimalist.com/helping-others-succeed/

Louise Veres (n. d) The Importance of Time Management: 8 Ways It Can Increase Your Success. https://thecentreforleadingandliving.ca/the-importance-of-time-management-8-ways-it-can-increase-your-success/

Pablo Diaz (November 12, 2015) No One Makes It Alone. https://www.guideposts.org/better-living/life-advice/finding-life-purpose/no-one-makes-it-alone

Carl Pullein (February 21, 2018) Why Time Management Is The Foundation Of A Successful Life. https://medium.com/carl-pullein/why-time-management-is-the-foundation-of-a-successful-life-275a998457cb

Max Palmer (July 22, 2019) How Time Management Plays A Major Role In Your Success. https://www.calendar.com/blog/how-time-management-plays-a-major-role-in-your-success/

Tony Robbins (n. d) Giving back to the community. https://www.tonyrobbins.com/giving-back/importance-giving-back/

John Jantsch (n. d) What Problem Does Your Business Solve For You?. https://ducttapemarketing.com/your-business-problem/

Ahmed Faraz (May 12, 2020) 10 Laws of Consistency | How to Stay Consistent at Anything in Life. https://www.onlinelifeguide.com/how-to-stay-consistent/

Merna (February 19th, 2020) How To Develop Consistency in 5 Steps. https://doinglifedifferently.com/how-to-develop-consistency-in-5-steps/

BetterAuds Team (n. d) 7 Secrets of Success that can change your life. https://betterauds.com/success/secrets-of-success-that-can-change-your-life/

Chad Halvorson (Oct 12, 2015) 11 habits of people who always reach their goals. https://www.businessinsider.com/11-habits-of-people-who-always-reach-their-goals-2015-10?r=US&IR=T

WorkForce Software (Jul 24, 2017) How to be Consistent. https://www.workforcesoftware.com/blog/how-to-be-consistent/

Nitin Shah (November 11, 2019) Consistency is the Key to Success: 6 Simple, actionable tips to develop consistency.

https://www.instituteofclinicalhypnosis.com/self-help/consistency-is-the-key-to-success/

Eric Holtzclaw (n. d) Power of Consistency: 5 Rules. https://www.inc.com/eric-v-holtzclaw/consistency-power-success-rules.html

Workopolis (May 15, 2015) The 5 people you need to succeed. https://careers.workopolis.com/advice/the-5-people-you-need-to-succeed/

Vincent Egoro (October 2, 2015) No Matter Who You Are, You Still Need Others To Succeed. https://vincentegoroblog.wordpress.com/2015/10/02/no-matter-who-you-are-you-still-need-others-to-succeed/